# THE SIXTH GREAT AWAKENING

*And the Coming Renewal of the American Church*

I

# What leaders are saying about The Sixth Great Awakening . . .

*"This is a refreshingly hopeful and well-reasoned book that counters the false narratives of a dying church. The church is the primary agency God uses to expand His kingdom here on earth; and you and I can be a part of the next great awakening."*

—DOUG CLAY, General Superintendent, General Council of the Assemblies of God (USA.)

*Joe Castleberry's sensational--yes, sensational--book opens a whole new vista into the future of Christian faith in America. Despite alarming statistics indicating the disappearance of religion and piety in public and private lives, the author also marshals convincing evidence showing the emergence and growth of the next cycle of revival. Critically applying generational theory, the book learns lessons from the ebb and flow of religion in American history. Coupled with biblical narratives, results from the most current research, and "pious imagination," Joe projects into the near future a most promising scenario of the next rise of Christian faith in this land.*

—REV., PROF. VELI-MATTI KÄRKKÄINEN Fuller Theological Seminary and University of Helsinki

*"The* Sixth Great Awakening *provides a historically*

*and biblically substantiated expectation for a sweeping spiritual awakening. All the major indicators and spiritual, political, and cultural drivers point to a fresh outpouring of God's Spirit that will result in the greatest harvest of souls in human history thus far."*

—SAMUEL RODRIGUEZ, President
National Hispanic Christian Leadership
Conference (NHCLC) and author of Your Mess,
God's Miracle

*I love this book! While pundits continue to moan the decline of the church and religious faith, The Sixth Great Awakening offers a contrary view of hope for a future revival. The author, Joseph Castleberry, integrates his extensive study of awakenings, generational theory, philosophy, and theology in a powerful analysis of our challenging times. His conclusion? An awakening is coming! Amen. May the Lord bring it soon.*

—GARY L. McINTOSH Sr. PhD, DMin,
author, speaker, and distinguished affiliate
professor
Talbot School of theology, Biola University

*"Dr. Castleberry's new book cogently explains the idea that the pendulum of irreligiousness has started its way back to God, heralding a fresh wave of faith. A well-researched and hopeful text."*
—CARLOS CAMPO, PhD, CEO, Museum of the Bible

*"A well-documented historic journey with often little-known facts that outlines that God has been*

*consistently and faithfully bringing revival and awakenings throughout generations. He also shows the long-lasting implications for our time. This wonderfully written book is engaging and brings us solid HOPE that God is at work!"*

—GREGORY JANTZ. PhD, C.E.D.S.
Founder, the Center - A Place of HOPE and author of *The Anxiety Reset: A Life-Changing Approach to Overcoming Fear, Stress, Worry, Panic Attacks, OCD, and More.*

*"At once historical and prophetic,* The Sixth Great Awakening *is a must-read for all those who care about revival and a future awakening."*

—*ELIEZER OYOLA, Ph.D, Professor Emeritus* of Spanish Language and Literature, Evangel University

"The Sixth Great Awakening *gives much-needed perspective and hope for such a time of tumult across America. History has shown us how God has restored America. Why not again?"*

—*TIP FRANK Founder, The 1776 Prayer Project*

*"Joe Castleberry combines fascinating research with powerful insights, providing not only a thorough understanding of our cultural moment but also a hope-filled expectation for the revival God is bringing. This book will help you to grasp how God has worked in the past and what He is doing in the present. This is*

*an incredible resource!"*

—*JOHN LINDELL,* Lead Pastor, James River Church

*Contrary to the messages of doom and gloom we so frequently hear about the decline of Christianity in the United States,* The Sixth Great Awakening *presents a robust case for hope. Grounded in solid sociological, theological, historical, and biblical research, Castleberry shows that the church has gone through five previous cycles of decline and renewal, always to emerge stronger than ever. As a pastor, trying to lead a church amidst the "great dechurching," I found the book's list of the signs of impending revival both hopeful and helpful. While revival is always about an outpouring of the Holy Spirit that we can't control, there are, nonetheless, things we can do as individuals and as Christian leaders to set the table for it.*

—SCOTT DUDLEY, Lead Pastor
Bellevue Presbyterian Church

# Other Books by Joseph Castleberry

*40 Days of Christmas: Celebrating the Glory of our Savior,* BroadStreet Publishing, 2018.

*The New Pilgrims: How Immigrants are Renewing America's Faith*, Worthy Publishing, 2015.

*The Kingdom Net: Learning to Network Like Jesus,* My Healthy Church, 2013.

*Your Deepest Dream: Discovering God's True Vision for Your Life*, NavPress, 2012.

# The Sixth Great Awakening

*And the Coming Renewal
of the American Church*

*Joseph Castleberry*

**Northwest**
UNIVERSITY | PRESS

© 2024 by Joseph Castleberry
Published by Northwest University Press
Kirkland, Washington

Library of Congress Cataloguing-in-Publication Data

Name: Castleberry, Joseph, author
Title: The Sixth Great Awakening and the Coming Renewal of the American Church / Joseph Castleberry
Description: first edition. Kirkland, Washington: Northwest University Press, 2024. Includes biographical references
Identifiers: ISBN: 9798333321732
Subjects: Revival, Awakenings, Generational Theory, Christianity, Christian Church Growth, Christian Spiritual Growth, Ministry Leadership. Prayer, Evangelism, Christian Inspiration

Cover design by Amy St. Clair.

Dedicated to Joseph Wiley Castleberry, Joseph Colombus Castleberry, and James Jackson Castleberry—three past generations of my family who hungered for God's presence in revival and received the awakenings of their time with joy and gratitude and hard work for the Kingdom— and for the generations ahead who will rescue the United States of America from ruin by their passion for the love of God, the grace of Christ, and the fellowship of the Holy Spirit.

# CONTENTS

# PREFACE

*Christendom has had a series of revolutions and in each one of them, Christianity has died. Christianity has died many times and risen again, for it had a God who knew the way out of the grave.*—G. K. Chesterton, *The Everlasting Man*

The Old Testament transparently depicts the fact that faith in the land of Israel waxed and waned continuously from the time of Abraham until the time of the restoration from captivity, and the Intertestamental Period (early Judaism) also shows times of backsliding and revival. As much as we might like to pretend that the outpouring of the Holy Spirit on the Day of Pentecost changed everything, the New Testament also tells of the instability of human performance in faith. The Seven Churches of Asia in Revelation 2-3 give several case studies in church vitality or decline, and the history of the Church since then has always featured both retraction and revival. In some formerly Christian countries of North Africa, Islam completely wiped out the indigenous Christians, and even the Christian population of

1

the Holy Land itself continues to shrink under Islamic pressure.

But Chesterton's lemma holds: Christianity always revives, resurrects, and lives to fight another day until the final victory of God appears. The story of Christianity in America displays a continuous cycle of dying and reviving, as America began in the midst of a religious awakening and has experienced five major seasons of renewal at the societal level over the course of its history. While we often think of the early years of the American colonies as times of great religious commitment because of what we have always heard about the Mayflower Pilgrims, who came to America as part of what might be called the Puritan Awakening, that fervor did not last, and religion in the colonies decayed over time, creating a need for another Awakening in 1725 (known as the "First" Great Awakening. After twenty years of awakening, faith once again began to wane. By the time of the Revolutionary War, the new nation faced a real spiritual crisis. The great historian of revival, J. Edwin Orr, described the time after the Revolutionary War as follows:

> Not many people realize that in the wake of the American Revolution (following 1776-1781) there was a moral slump. Drunkenness became epidemic. Out of a population of five million, 300,000 were confirmed drunkards; Profanity was of the most shocking kind. For the first time in

the history of the American settlement, women were afraid to go out at night for fear of assault. Bank robberies were a daily occurrence. What about the churches? The Methodists were losing more members than they were gaining. The Baptists said that they had their most wintry season. The Presbyterians in general assembly deplored the nation's ungodliness. In a typical Congregational church, the Rev. Samuel Shepherd of Lennox, Massachusetts, in sixteen years had not taken one young person into fellowship. The Lutherans were so languishing that they discussed uniting with Episcopalians who were even worse off. The Protestant Episcopal Bishop of New York, Bishop Samuel Provost, quit functioning; he had confirmed no one for so long that he decided he was out of work, so he took up other employment. The Chief Justice of the United States, John Marshall, wrote to the Bishop of Virginia, James Madison, that the Church 'was too far gone ever to be redeemed.' Voltaire averred and Tom Paine echoed, 'Christianity will be forgotten in thirty years.[1]

Yet from the brink of disaster, in 1801 America began to experience the Second Great Awakening with the Cane Ridge Revival Kentucky, and Christianity rose again to great heights of influence.

Today, we see real trouble in America's churches, and many wonder whether Christianity can survive. I believe that we will not only survive, but we will see our greatest numerical growth, our greatest season of anointing, and our most important time of influence in the next 30 to 40 years—if Jesus tarries. **Impressive revivals will come to American churches over the next 25 years, setting the stage for the next Great Awakening—the sixth such Awakening in American history.** We have a good theoretical basis for predicting it, and American history richly illustrates it. And Christians throughout the country believe that revival is coming and pray earnestly for it. We should expect incredible showers of blessing in the next 20 years. The Church will revive because that is what the church does, because that is what the Lord of the Church did.

# CHAPTER 1

# GLIMPSING THE BEGINNINGS OF AN AWAKENING

The Church in America has suffered a truly "wintry season" over the past twenty years. Faith retention among Christian youth across all expressions of the Church has dropped to the lowest levels ever recorded, with as many as 70% of Christian youths from Evangelical, Mainline Protestant, and Roman Catholic churches at least temporarily abandoning their churches after high school.[2] Nevertheless, that awful statistic finds a measure of consolation in the fact that many young people return to faith and church in their twenties and thirties.  In 2019, Lifeway Research estimated a 70% retention rate for Protestants.[3] In the past, 90% of Christian youth typically retained their faith.[4]  Nothing could threaten the Church (nor disturb the hearts of believing parents) more than the pattern of losing 30% of our children to unbelief!

A companion statistic to faith loss involves what Pew Research called "the Rise of the Nones."[5] For a period of over twenty years, we have seen a rise of 1% per year in the percentage of Americans reporting their religious affiliation as "none," to the point that 28% of Americans now report no particular faith position.[6] National Public Radio reported in 2024 that:

> A new study from Pew Research finds that the religiously unaffiliated – a group comprised of atheists, agnostics and those who say their religion is "nothing in particular"—is now the largest cohort in the U.S. They're more prevalent among American adults than Catholics (23%) or evangelical Protestants (24%).[7]

Indeed, the Church in America has seen dark days since we experienced the COVID-19 Pandemic.  Many churches rejoice in  the fact that they actually grew during the time of COVID and others have seen remarkable recovery since the end of masking.  But overall,

Church attendance has rebounded a little—perhaps only in a rounding error—since the end of the pandemic, with 28% of U.S. adults in March 2023 reporting that they had attended religious services in person in the last month, compared to 27% in March 2022 and 26% in September 2021.[8] Such numbers compare to 42% attending *weekly* twenty years ago.[9]

Many grim predictions have resulted as social scientists and Christian leaders have tried to account for the future by extrapolating these losses forward.[10] But such predictions will always err because they have not factored in the inherent hunger for God in human beings and the power of God, whom nothing can stop from saving, whether by many or by few (1 Samuel 14:6). No matter how moribund the Church may appear, God can turn things around quickly. Only time will tell how God will intervene to achieve the plan of salvation and the glorious presentation of the triumphant Church without spot or wrinkle. **But American churches should experience remarkable revivals and growth over the next twenty years before seeing the dawning of the Sixth Great Awakening in the 2040s.**

Already, glimpses of an Awakening flicker ahead of us. According to Aaron Earls of Lifeway Research, "Most major religious demographic studies now show a decline or, at the very least, a plateauing of the religiously unaffiliated in the U.S:

On the low end, Gallup has had Nones hovering between 20-21% since 2017. The **General Social Survey** (GSS) noted its first percentage drop among Nones, from 29% to 27%, in 2022. **Pew Research** recorded a decline from 31% to 28% in 2023. The **Cooperative Election Study** (CES), the only survey previously indicating growth among the religiously unaffiliated, has now tracked a leveling off between 34% and 36% from 2020 to 2023.[11]

Astute observers will note variation among these sources about the percentage of "nones" in America, but this shows evidence of how slippery the category can be, depending on the phrasing of questions. Nevertheless, the consistency of the different sources clearly suggests a slight decline in the number of religiously unaffiliated people in America. Has the Church begun to climb out of its decline?

**Awakening among Classical Liberals**

Another ray of hope for an Awakening twinkles in a remarkable and surprising new redevelopment hat has begun among leading public intellectuals who identify as classical liberals. To understand the significance of this emerging phenomenon, we have to discuss the rise of the New Atheism movement, which began about 20 years ago with the publication in 2004 of

Sam Harris' book, *The End of Faith: Religion, Terror, and the Future of Reason.*

Featuring thinkers like Richard Dawkins, Sam Harris, Christopher Hitchens, and Ayaan Hirsi Ali, the New Atheism rejected religion as irrational and actually harmful to society—a thesis motivated in part by the horrific Wahabist terrorist attacks on New York and Washington on September 11. The powerful, charismatic personalities leading the New Atheism made the movement very attractive to many young people. Despite a great deal of popular success, the movement came under criticism from many philosophers and classical liberal public intellectuals—as well as scientists—for its lack of philosophical rigor. Nevertheless, New Atheism had a role in increasing the number of atheists in America and in the "rise of the nones."

**Hope Rises as Public Intellectuals Return to Church**

In contrast to the recent increase in doubt and unbelief, a new religious movement has begun in the past five years or so among classical liberals. Classical liberals, in contrast to today's left-wing postmodernist progressives who promote an ideology that reduces social relations to the oppressed-oppressor binary and promote "cancel culture," treasure the traditional Western liberal values of economic freedom (free markets) and personal liberties (freedoms of thought and speech and civil rights). A simple way of thinking about classical liberals would bring up the memory of Democrats like Harry Truman and John F. Kennedy and Republicans like Dwight D. Eisenhower and Ronald Reagan.

Considered "moderates" today, classical liberals find themselves repulsed by "illiberal" cancel culture and the rise of anti-white, anti-Semitic, and anti-Asian racial discrimination in the name of anti-racism, and they have begun to reconsider their alliance with left-wing liberals or "progressives." An increasing number of liberals have concluded that the rejection of Judeo-Christian values in Western societies has left them with no solid basis for their liberal moral sentiments and convictions, which originated specifically in Judaism and Christianity and find no real support in any other worldview. As a result, many liberals, including atheists, have reconsidered their views toward religion. While they still may not fully believe in God, they have come to see that liberal societies cannot function without religious communities.

The term "public intellectual" refers to scholars who choose to interact directly with society instead of directing all their communications to academic settings. In recent years, many liberal public intellectuals have begun to return to church and synagogue. Clinical psychologist Jordan Peterson became one of the most important "evangelists" in the world leading untold numbers of young adults back to faith and religious observance, mostly while refusing to say whether he actually believed in God or not.

Christopher Kaczor, co-author of *Jordan Peterson, God, and Christianity,* commenting about Peterson's widely popular teachings on the Bible, has said:

> "I read online comments from many atheists who said that before listening to his YouTube lectures on the Psychological Significance of the Biblical Stories: Genesis, they thought the Bible was a ridiculous old book that had nothing to teach the modern mind, but after they listened to [Peterson's] lectures, they concluded that the Book of Genesis, indeed the Bible as a whole, is an immensely rich and profound storehouse of wisdom for living today."[12]

The classical liberal intellectual and New York Times columnist—and recent Christian convert—David Brooks wrote, "My friend Tyler Cowen argues that Jordan Peterson is the most influential public intellectual in the Western world right now, and he has a point."[13] Peterson's wife Tammy and daughter Mikhaila have respectively converted to Catholic and Evangelical faith, even as Peterson continues to "wrestle with God." Mikhaila Peterson has established her own very popular podcast, where she speaks to a young and primarily secular audience openly about her faith in Jesus, the healing of her parents, and the presence of the Holy Spirit.[14]

Along the lines of C.S. Lewis' declaration that Jesus fits into the category of "true myth," standing in the line of other mythological dying-and-resurrected gods but having actually lived, Peterson tearfully confessed, "The problem is, I probably believe that. And I am amazed at my own belief, and I don't understand it."[15] But Peterson remains cautious in stating what he believes, perhaps purposefully allowing his audience to come to its own conclusion based on the ideas he presents. Although his method differs from classic Christian apologetics and evangelism, his approach seems to have a greater effect in leading today's younger generations to faith in God and Christ.

The atheist historian of classical antiquity, Tom Holland, may have become the world's ablest defender of the importance of Christianity for forming the values of Western society, and while he has not yet made a full confession of personal faith in Christ, he speaks powerfully and convincingly about the importance of faith as he inches closer and closer to the Church. Holland, explaining why he changed his mind about Christianity, explained that as a child,

*The glamour and beauty and power and the cruelty of the Greeks and Romans I found very appealing . . . I went to Sunday school and was very interested in biblical history as*

*well, but I found them all a bit po-faced, I didn't like their beards, I preferred the clean-shaven look of Apollo. In a way I was kind of seduced by the glamour of Greece and Rome, so the first books I wrote about history were about Greece and Rome.*

The more he studied classical history, however, the more appalled he became by the cruelty of these ancient civilizations and how utterly alien they seem in comparison to Western values. He found that the New Testament Scriptures introduced

"almost everything that explains the modern world and the way the West has then moved on to shape concepts like international law, concepts of human rights, all these kinds of things. Ultimately, they don't go back to Greek philosophers, they don't go back to Roman imperialism. They go back to Paul. His letters, I think, along with the four gospels, are the most influential, the most impactful, the most revolutionary writings that have emerged from the ancient world.

Holland says, "I began to realize that actually, in almost every way I am Christian."[16]

Holland continues to engage with Christians and their religious practices, even without fully surrendering his heart to Jesus. But the Holy Spirit does not need our assent to use us for God's glory! The widely celebrated economic historian, Sir Niall Ferguson, perhaps borrowing a phrase from the Russian-British satirist and social commentator Konstantin Kisin, now refers to himself as a "lapsed atheist who goes to church every Sunday."[17] It appears that Christian Atheism has become a real thing now, but one wonders whether in many cases it will merely serve as a way station on the road back to full Christian faith.[18]

One of the most surprising and powerful stories of conversion from atheism has recently come from Ferguson's wife, Ayaan Hirsi Ali, who made her fame as the "Fifth Horseman" of the New Atheist Movement.[19] Raised as a Muslim in Somalia, she fled from her native country to avoid a forced marriage, becoming a citizen of the Netherlands before running for office and gaining status as a popular member of the Dutch Parliament. Rejecting the Islamic faith, she became a famous atheist alongside Richard Dawkins, who became her mentor. When Islamic radicals threatened her life, she immigrated to the United States, where she married Ferguson, a fellow atheist and public intellectual.

Over time, she sunk into a terrible depression, wrestling daily with suicidal thoughts. She tried to treat it with "evidence-based science" to no avail. But in early 2023, when her psychotherapist suggested she was suffering from "spiritual bankruptcy," it resonated with her, and she decided to pray. "I prayed desperately," she said recently in a debate with Richard Dawkins in which she powerfully testified of her newfound faith, "and for me that was a turning point. What happened after that,

> was a miracle in its own right. I feel connected to something higher and greater than myself . . . My zest for life is back. That experience has filled me with humility, I have to say, and it is something that is very subjective. It is extremely difficult to explain, and I'm trying to get into the granular details of how I got there in a book."[20]

Another remarkable testimony that has emerged recently comes from the highly intelligent British comedian and podcaster Russell Brand. When he married singer Katy Perry twenty years ago, her parents—who were pastors—prophesied that he would become "a great man of God."[21] The marriage did not endure, and Brand went on to serious misadventures afterward, but his recent testimonies of conversion and baptism have demonstrated great sincerity and power. While many show business personalities convert publicly, only to disappoint the Church soon afterward, Brand's conversion suggests that not only intellectuals, but artists also are finding their way back to faith.

The list of classical liberals either returning

to church or recognizing the value of having faith or explicitly coming to faith goes on and on, but it certainly includes thinkers like the journalist and self-described "Christian atheist" Douglas Murray, the wildly popular podcaster Joe Rogan, and the Jewish journalist Bari Weiss, among others.[22]

**What Does This Mean?**

As a philosophy student in my undergraduate years, I observed that artists and philosophers do not create social movements. But they tend to see them emerging before everyone else does. It may take a decade or two for the rest of society to catch up with them or for their ideas to find expression in a social movement. Obviously, not all currents in intellectual or artistic life become massive social movements, but **this move back to church and synagogue by leading public intellectuals suggests that in the years to come, the average citizen may arrive at the same conclusion: going to church offers great benefits to individuals, and a well-ordered society needs people's participation in religious communities in order to flourish.**

It does not suffice for each of us to commit to "my truth." Societies require people to commit themselves to "our truth." And further, "our truth" must correspond to reality and to human nature for it to serve as a unifying element for the flourishing of a society. When a whole society commits itself to false ideas, as we have seen especially in the past twenty years, disaster ensues. But as people go back to church, most of them will find their way back to God. And God remains the answer to America's problems. In any case, thought leaders have started to return to church and to God. **Will a social movement—the Sixth Great Awakening—come soon as more and more people wake up to the truth that our society has set a course toward shipwreck?** We don't know. But we should pray!

While the conversion of public intellectuals offers an exciting preview of a future awakening, the argument here primarily focuses primarily on another source of hope: the cyclical theory of history proposed by William and Neil Howe. Known as Strauss-Howe Generational Theory, it offers a powerful interpretation of American history that suggests that America should enter an Awakening in the 2040s. Read on to see why.

# CHAPTER 2

# THE SIXTH GREAT AWAKENING

A new Great Awakening will dawn in America sometime in the next 25 years. Imagine how a future e-zine feature story might read:

*No one in government or the media expected what has happened in America over the past decade. Older people compare this new phenomenon to the "Jesus Movement" of the 1960's. This new social movement began among college students at the University of Washington and at high schools throughout the region when students began to flood into local churches. They returned to their schools with testimonies of transformed lives and new identities after an encounter with Jesus Christ. The phenomenon quickly sprang up in cities and universities across the country as hundreds, and then thousands of young people followed them back to church. But Christians say that the movement really had its roots in revivals that occurred in their churches in the previous years, resulting in hundreds of young people being called to the ministry and prepared to lead "the next great awakening."*

*What began as a religious revival among college students has replicated across the country and has begun to have a noticeable effect on society and culture. The marriage rate has soared; the number of children born out of wedlock has plummeted. Churches have filled up to the point that even the smallest churches host multiple services. Counseling centers close their doors as Americans report less and less depression and anxiety. Large crowds fill stadiums across the nation for city-wide worship services and evangelistic events. Homelessness continues to disappear from the streets as governments partner with churches and Christian non-profit organizations to provide successful solutions to what seemed like an intractable problem just a few years ago. Crime rates have decreased to historic lows.*

*Even once secularist corporate offices*

*have seen Bible studies meeting at lunch time in their cafeterias and conference rooms. Prayer meetings have become popular everywhere. While traditional media outlets initially greeted the movement with harsh critique, the voices of thousands of social media journalists spread the news widely. Eventually, the traditional media had no choice but to start reporting on the movement objectively and even positively. Their audiences now demand coverage of the daily news stories that break from churches and religious organizations. Even the detractors seem fascinated with the stories of transformation, healing, and community service that keep emerging.*

*Church weddings have become the rage as millions have made churches their central source of community. Likewise, parenting has become a hot topic in the news as more couples decide to have children and need advice in raising them. Most congregations sponsor events six nights a week to minister to the different population groups (men, women, teens, children, singles, outreach teams) that carry out their ministry. Young people, as well as older adults, have abandoned secular employment to go into the ministry. Church ministry classes at Bible colleges and seminaries report full classrooms.*

*Along with the rise in religious practice has come a generalized interest in a deeper understanding of life, with a marked increase in interest in music and the arts. Colleges and universities have seen an increase in students seeking to major in fields such as history, literature, religion, classical languages, and philosophy. Whereas colleges had become more practical, narrowly educating students for specific professional and technical jobs, more and more students express a thirst for truth and a desire for greater meaning in their lives.*

**Scholars say it is the most dramatic religious awakening in American history...**

---

## Revival Now

Such a scenario may seem far-fetched to many, but it represents the future many Christians most fondly dream of. Hopes recently spiked when news quickly spread about a remarkable visitation of the Holy Spirit at Asbury University between February 8 and 24 in 2023. The revival set expectations ablaze among Christians across the United States and around the world with the burning question, "Is it time for the next Great Awakening?" Hoping for the fire to spread, college ministers and students began to seek God for revival, with large baptism events and extended worship services breaking out across the country.

Nevertheless, the Asbury Revival did not immediately give birth to a new Great Awakening . . . yet. College students and campus ministers and people hungry for revival continue to offer evidence that the next great move of God has already begun but has not yet started spreading widely. Expectations wax and wane, from place to place, according to our own sense of hunger for and faith in the God who nothing can hinder from saving (1 Samuel 14:6).

The Book of Hebrews begins with the words, *"In the past God spoke to our ancestors through the prophets at many times and in various ways"* before declaring Jesus as God's ultimate declaration. The phrase *"at many times and in various ways"* aptly describes God's usual way of working in the world. God continues to work in the world, here and there, in large ways and small, whether or not we see a massive revival or a great awakening. And in God's time, great things happen that change the course of history. None of them have the kind of effect that the coming of Christ had, nor can any of them bring the Second Coming. But whenever God visits his people, lives change and families, communities, and even nations receive renewed hope and a future.

As the title of this book suggests, I believe America will begin to experience its Sixth Great Awakening sometime in the next 25 years. Church historians have spoken of two Great Awakenings, although some argue that there has only been one such Awakening, the so-called second one.[23] In short, we can let the academic historians argue about such things, as they make their living by disagreeing with each other. In fact, no objective definition exists to determine what qualifies as a "Great Awakening." Whatever we may call it, the First Great Awakening featured revivals dramatic enough to affect our view of history three hundred years later.

On the other hand, it does not really figure as the first Awakening in America, as America was born in the Puritan Awakening in England that sent the Pilgrims and Puritans on their great religious mission to America between 1620 and 1646. According to the definition of an Awakening proposed by William Strauss and Neil Howe, America has experienced five Awakenings over the past 400 years of its history: the Puritan Awakening (1621-1649); the First Great Awakening (1727-1746); the Transcendental or "Second Great" Awakening (1822-1844, although I would date it as 1800-1824)[24]; the Missionary/ Pentecostal Awakening (1886-1908); and the Consciousness Revolution or the Jesus Movement (1964-1984).

Having grown up in the revivalist tradition of American Evangelicalism, I have sought revival throughout my life, experiencing the fifth Awakening as a child, teenager, and young adult when the Jesus Movement and the Charismatic Movement brought millions of Americans to faith in God and participation in churches between the 1960s and the Eighties. I also lived in Latin America during the successive waves of that Awakening and visited the Pensacola Revival in Florida during the 1990s, extending my experience with spectacular revival and church growth.

Many Baby Boomers like me long for the "good old days" of revival with all our hearts. Members of subsequent generations who love the Lord may have never experienced revival, even at the local church level, but they have heard the reports of the older believers of what revival brought, how it felt, and how things should work. As the prophet wrote,

> Lord, I have heard of your fame;
> I stand in awe of your deeds, Lord.
> Repeat them in our day,
> in our time make them known;
> in wrath remember mercy. (Habakkuk 3:1)

and as the Psalmist lamented:

> We have heard it with our ears, O God;
> our ancestors have told us
> what you did in their days,
> in days long ago . . .
> Rise up and help us;
> rescue us because of your unfailing
> love. (Psalm 44:1, 26)

Christians today still call out to God to send a revival, to shake the world once again, to save our generation, and to make God's Glory known.

## Defining an Awakening

The definition of an Awakening, as it has emerged in certain social and historical analyses in recent years, provides a crucial element in the argument here.[25] Many people use the words "revival" and "awakening" as synonyms, perhaps seeing awakening as a more widespread revival. But the argument here requires sharper definitions. Spiritual resurgence happens at three levels: personal, local, and societal. When an individual experiences *spiritual renewal*, it may have little effect beyond the personal level, although it usually affects his or her direct relationships. When a personal spiritual renewal occurs, whether in conversion or in a subsequent experience of refreshed faith, people find a new love for God, a new sense of intimacy with Christ through the Holy Spirit who fills their life, a new hunger for the Word of God, and a desire to speak to others about their new or renewed experience with God. Such a personal renewal can change a life forever, but it does not necessarily set off a revival.

A *revival* occurs when a group of people—whether a local church, a Bible study, or even a group of school friends—experiences a spiritual renewal together. Their meetings feature a perceptible move of God that anyone visiting would recognize as special or unusual. Not only do the people involved in the revival experience a renewed love and passion for God, but that renewal affects their activities as a group. They begin to share their experience with family and friends, who visit their group meetings (e.g., church services) and catch the same enthusiasm for God. Unbelievers have an encounter with God that changes their lives, and people around them begin to take notice and even start going to meetings with them, where they also encounter the reality of God.

Such revivals can last for days or weeks or years—even decades—and they may draw thousands of visitors. Revivalist Christians always keep their bags packed, at least mentally, waiting for a chance to visit a revival and experience the "manifest presence of God." While people know an omnipresent God inhabits the whole creation and can move on them anywhere, they hunger for immediate, palpable experiences of God's glorious presence. Thousands of people travelled to the remote country town of Wilmore, Kentucky to experience the recent revival at Asbury University, overwhelming the small town's infrastructure.

Like storm chasers who track and try to anticipate the trajectory of a tornado to experience the emotional rush of being in the midst of awesome power, some Christians will drop everything as quickly as possible to experience the manifest power of God. Their enthusiasm draws criticism from some observers, but not generally from people who have experienced God that way in the past.

Revivals can and do happen at any time, regardless of whether society presents conditions that seem "ripe" for revival. **They break out when people seek God with all their hearts and pray for revival.** As God said to Israel while sending them into exile,

> ... *I know the plans I have for you . . . plans to prosper you and not to harm you, plans to give you hope and a future.* **Then you will call on me and come and pray to me, and I will listen to you. You will seek me and find me when you seek me with all your heart.** *I will be found by you . . . and will bring you back from captivity.* (Jeremiah 29:11-14)

We should understand these popularly cited verses primarily in the historical context in which Jeremiah delivered them—the midst of rolling exile. By no means do they constitute a blanket promise of prosperity for all people at all times, but to the contrary, an assurance of restoration *after* hard times. They do, however, represent the character of a merciful and forgiving God.

One of Israel's most ancient and most repeated credal statements, pronounced by the very voice of God to Moses, declares:

> *The Lord, the Lord, a God merciful and gracious, slow to anger, and abounding in steadfast love and faithfulness, keeping steadfast love for thousands, forgiving iniquity and transgression and sin, but who*

> *will by no means clear the guilty, visiting the*
> *iniquity of the fathers on the children and*
> *the children's children, to the third and the*
> *fourth generation.* (Exodus 34:6-7)

Notice in these verses the intergenerational effect of sin.  But the converse also holds:  God will bless the generations of families that seek God's face.

Another important passage further declares God's forgiving nature: *If my people, who are called by my name, will humble themselves and pray and seek my face and turn from their wicked ways, then I will hear from heaven, and I will forgive their sin and will heal their land* (2 Chronicles 7:14).  While Solomon received this promise at the dedication of the Temple, foretelling future backsliding in Israel and assuring God's continuing willingness to forgive, it reveals an essential element of God's nature.  Whenever the people of God turn to God in repentance, and seek God in prayer with all their hearts, they can rest assured that, sooner or later, God will show them mercy and steadfast love, revealing his Holy Presence to them in the power of the Holy Spirit, and reviving them for God's glory.

A revival does not constitute an *Awakening*. Awakenings occur society-wide and break out spontaneously in a wide variety of places.  No one place constitutes the "center" of the Awakening; it seemingly occurs in many places simultaneously. Revivals in local churches and in larger circles can occur as God responds to the prayers of people, but it takes a whole society to produce an Awakening, and it happens when the pursuit of success and prosperity inevitably fails to bring fulfillment. When material things fail to satisfy the longings of the human heart, people will finally get around to looking deeper. When a whole society develops a spiritual hunger, younger generations turn their attention to the arts, take up great moral causes, build better communities, and return to or seek out new religious pursuits.

**An Awakening—as a human sociological phenomenon rather than a "sovereign work of God's grace"—does not necessarily result in church growth or conversions to Christianity.** President John F. Kennedy popularized an old New England aphorism in a speech given in 1963: "A rising tide lifts all boats."[26] While the saying usually shows up in economic speeches, the principle also applies to an Awakening. When a society begins to yearn for spiritual values, all forms of spirituality start getting attention. During an Awakening, churches will grow, but mosques, synagogues, Hindu temples, Buddhist meditation sites and other religious and spiritual institutions and groups also tend to prosper. Secular forms of spirituality also grow.

The Awakening of the late 1960s, Seventies, and Eighties not only featured the Jesus Movement and the Charismatic Movement, but also the rise of Eastern religions, the Hare Krishna movement, and the secular spirituality (or pseudo-spirituality) of the hippie movement, with its free love and psychedelic drug experiments. **No law of history or sociology requires an Awakening to result in the exclusive growth of Christianity over and against all other options. If the Church does not shine during an Awakening, great opportunity for the salvation of nations can go to waste.**

The notion of a secular spirituality may not sound familiar to Evangelical Christians, but such a thing does exist. The postmodern social justice movement in recent years, with its concepts of white privilege, white guilt, racism as America's original sin, and other quasi-religious concepts has widely been described as a secularized version of Christian morality. Referred to frequently as "the Great Awokening" by both conservative and liberal observers, the movement clearly addresses the needs of its followers to establish a sense of personal righteousness in the midst of societal iniquity.[27] Liberal intellectual Matthew Yglesias compares the movement to the Second Great Awakening and its abolitionist movement.[28] Jonathan Chait has proclaimed that the Great Awokening is over, but speculates that a second Trump presidency could revive it.[29] As an inherently political spirituality, even the mention of it stirs controversy and division among Christians.

Throughout human history, societal

awakenings have led to the birth and growth of many religions. For example, the rise of Islam occurred during an Arabian Awakening in the Seventh Century A.D. New religions, sects, or cults also thrive in an Awakening. Seventh Day Adventism, an orthodox Christian sect, arose during the Second Great Awakening (1801-1824). So did the more radically new and not-so-orthodox Church of Jesus Christ of Latter-Day Saints. The Jehovah's Witness religion arose during the Missionary/Pentecostal Awakening (1886-1908). *A season of awakening does not guarantee that Christianity will prosper, but it does offer a remarkable opportunity for renewal and growth.*

*Indeed, in some countries that once thrived with Christian revival and growth, other religions have replaced Christianity.* As an example, Turkey —famous for the Seven Churches of Asia in the Book of Revelation and the Byzantine Church— fell under the control of Islam in the seventh and eighth centuries (A.D.) and barely even tolerates Christianity today. Contemporary post-Christian Europe offers as an example of what can happen when churches do not thrive and grow during times of societal opportunity. While America experienced the Jesus Movement during the last Awakening, European Christianity languished in the wake of the disaster of World War II, in which so-called Christian countries almost annihilated each other. The way churches respond to an

Awakening has a lot to do with whether they will make the most of a propitious opportunity or lose out. The final chapter of this book will offer advice for taking the best advantage of the next Awakening.

America has actually experienced five periods of twenty years or more that could properly classify as Awakenings or even "great awakenings." As mentioned before, following Strauss-Howe Generational Theory, I identify those Awakenings as the Puritan Awakening (1621-1649); the First Great Awakening (1727-1746); the Second Great Awakening (1801-1824)[30]; the Missionary/Pentecostal Awakening (1886-1908); and the Jesus Movement/ Charismatic Movement (1964-1984).[31] The next Awakening—the sixth such phenomenon in American history—should begin sometime in the next 20 to 25 years.

Our nation came into being during (and at least partly as a result of) an Awakening in England at the time of our Pilgrim and Puritan immigrant ancestors (and no matter whether one can trace his or her ancestry to them or has just recently arrived in America from the remotest part of the world, those early pioneers count as the intellectual and spiritual ancestors of all Americans). America experienced what historians call the "First" Great Awakening in 1725, the first "home-grown" Awakening that established the spiritual paradigm for the history of revival in our country.

The Second Great Awakening dawned in 1801, resulting in the planting of thousands of churches and re-establishing the dominance of Christianity in the American psyche that Alexis de Tocqueville recognized on his famous visit to America in the 1830s. In the 1880s, the Missionary Awakening began, which would not only result in millions of conversions in America but also the Student Volunteer Movement, which resulted in the sending of over 20,000 long-term, cross-cultural missionaries from America to foreign fields.[32] The Missionary Awakening and its underlying holiness movement contributed to the greatest period of growth in Christian history in every corner of the globe as well as giving birth to the Pentecostal-Charismatic Movement. The latter set off successive waves of revival that have spread to the point of becoming the second largest category of Christians in the world (after Roman Catholicism). The fifth awakening in American history started in the 1960s with the explosion of the Jesus Movement and the Charismatic Movement, which the recent movie, "Jesus Revolution," chronicled and depicted with stunning accuracy and power.[33]

As readers may have noticed, an Awakening has occurred about every eighty years throughout American history. That may seem like bad news to Baby Boomer Christians like me who may not live to see another such a time of potential great victory for the Church. But in truth, it offers hope and a great challenge for everyone living today! As we move closer and closer to that Awakening, individuals will experience personal renewals that will set them in place as leaders of what God will do. Churches will experience revivals to prepare them to reap the coming harvest—the greatest ingathering of souls the world has ever seen, and perhaps the greatest it will ever see. We will plant thousands of churches in the years ahead.

The work God has cut out for the American Church will truly thrill and amaze us. And just as the Baby Boomers enjoyed the privilege of playing on the stage in the last Awakening, the latest-born and longest-lived of them will have a great seat in the balcony for the next Awakening, from which they will applaud and encourage and advise and pray for their children, grandchildren and great grandchildren as younger generations play the leading roles in God's great drama of redemption.

Will the next time of spiritual searching bring a "great Awakening" like the five previous ones in which Christianity thrived and millions of Americans turned to personal faith in Jesus Christ and membership in America's churches, or will the next Awakening give rise to other forms of spirituality and not a rebound of Christian spirituality? It depends on whether God has finished with us and does not pour out a sovereign work of grace to revive the American Church. It also depends on whether American Christians will seek God's face "with all their heart" (Jeremiah 29:14).

The next chapter will lay out a generational theory of history that offers an explanation for why such regularity occurs. But if the patterns of history hold, we can expect America's Sixth Great Awakening to break out between 2040 and 2045—although it certainly can occur earlier than that. Regardless of when the next Awakening arrives, God will have prepared us for it through an extremely fruitful period of preparation for God's people over the next twenty years. American churches and Christians should expect great things in the challenging-but-glorious years ahead so they can get ready for the blessings—and the work that will come.

# CHAPTER 3

# GENERATIONAL THEORY AND THE NEXT AWAKENING

The generation that came of age in the late 1960s demonstrated a sharp rejection of their parents' values, complete with sexual promiscuity, psychedelic drug experimentation, anti-war protests, the hippie lifestyle, long hair, and outlandish apparel. A defining concept for that era emerged when Look Magazine editor John Poppy introduced the phrase "generation gap" in 1967 to describe the growing rift between young people and their parents.[34]    The gap seemed radical in those days, perhaps even more radical than the generation gap that separates today's multiple generations.  But generations have always experienced the world differently throughout human history.

One of the key questions about time considers whether it proceeds in a linear direction or a cyclical repetition.  Some cultures primarily see time as cyclical, but Western societies, following the Bible, primarily understand it as a linear progression.  The Scriptures not only tell us that God, in the beginning, created the heavens and the earth (Genesis 1:1), but they also foretell the end of time and of the whole creation.  Peter wrote, describing the end of the world:

*The day of the Lord will come like a thief. The heavens will disappear with a roar; the elements will be destroyed by fire, and the earth and everything done in it will be laid bare. Since everything will be destroyed in this way, what kind of people ought you to be? You ought to live holy and godly lives as you look forward to the day of God and speed its coming. That day will bring about the destruction of the heavens by fire, and the elements will melt in the heat. But in keeping with his promise we are looking forward to a new heaven and a new earth, where righteousness dwells* (2 Peter 3:11-13).

Similarly, John the Revelator declares:

> *Then I saw "a new heaven and a new earth," for the first heaven and the first earth had passed away, and there was no longer any sea. I saw the Holy City, the new Jerusalem, coming down out of heaven from God, prepared as a bride beautifully dressed for her husband. And I heard a loud voice from the throne saying, "Look! God's dwelling place is now among the people, and he will dwell with them. They will be his people, and God himself will be with them and be their God. 'He will wipe every tear from their eyes. There will be no more death' or mourning or crying or pain, for the old order of things has passed away"* (Revelation 21:1-4).

The Scriptures clearly indicate that time will come to an end, giving way to a day of eternal light that will never end. If time (and the created order that it belongs to) has a beginning and an end, then time is linear.

Nevertheless, time also appears undeniably cyclical. Every year the earth revolves around the sun, proceeding inerrantly through the seasons of spring, summer, fall, and winter. The order of the seasons repeats itself in an inherently changeless cycle.[35] But beyond the physical and natural cycles and processions of the seasons, humans have long believed that history repeats itself. Time is not merely linear. Even casual observation of human history suggests a series of seeming repetitions.

Time never runs backwards, and human affairs never look exactly the same way twice. Tradition, but no actual text we can discover, tells us that Mark Twain famously said, "History doesn't repeat itself, but it rhymes." Maybe he never said it, but one of his contemporaries, A. N. Mouravieff, wrote in 1845:

> The vision recurs; the eastern sun has a second rise; history repeats her tale unconsciously and goes off into a mystic rhyme; ages are prototypes of other ages, and the winding course of time brings us round to the same spot again.[36]

Karl Marx wrote, cynically, that the German idealist philosopher Hegel "remarks somewhere that all great world-historic facts and personages appear, so to speak, twice. He forgot to add: the first time as tragedy, the second time as farce."[37]

Whatever we make of the nature of time, we must recognize that human beings tend to repeat the same mistakes that others before them committed. As the Preacher wrote in Ecclesiastes,

> *What has been will be again, what has been done will be done again:*
> *There is nothing new under the sun.*
> *Is there anything of which one can*

> *say, "Look! This is something new"? It was*
> *here already, long ago; it was here before*
>
> *our time.* **No one remembers the former**
> **generations,** *and even those yet to come*
> *will not be remembered by those who*
> *follow them* (Ecclesiastes 1:9-11).

Rather than seeing time as linear or cyclical, it seems best to recognize that it moves forward in an ever-widening spiral, not exactly repeating itself but ever reminiscent of the patterns of the past. The radical growth of the human population combined with the incredible explosion of knowledge and technology in our time creates ever larger and more dramatic changes in society as history spirals forward like a Slinky, but one in which the spirals get larger and larger as time winds on.

As mentioned in Ecclesiastes, one of the most important segments of biblical time is the *generation*. Generations have always fascinated human beings, since hardly anything delights us more than the birth of our children and grandchildren and their children. Another key concept is the **age**. Biblically speaking, an age lasts for the time of a human lifespan. Psalm 90, traditionally ascribed to Moses in the ancient note at the beginning of the Psalm, speaks of generations and ages as follows:

> *Lord, you have been our dwelling place*
> *throughout all generations.*

> *Before the mountains were born or you brought forth the whole world, from everlasting to everlasting you are God . . . A thousand years in your sight are like a day that has just gone by, or like a watch in the night. Yet you sweep people away in the sleep of death—they are like the new grass of the morning . . . Our days may come to seventy years, or eighty, if our strength endures; yet the best of them are but trouble and sorrow, for they quickly pass, and we fly away* (Psalm 90:1-2, 4-5, 10).

The Psalmist suggests here that a human age lasts 70-80 years. A new generation comes to birth every 20-30 years. Multiple generations live at the same time (often four or even five, since some humans live to 100 years of age), and they have always struggled to understand each other.

The Hebrews referred to an age or lifetime as one's "days" (*yomim*). The Greeks spoke of the *aion*, and the Romans used the term "*saeculum*"—all meaning (among other things) the span of a human life, which they generally considered to last 70 to 100 years.[38] In speaking of eternity or forever, the New Testament refers to "the ages of the ages"—meaning "for all of the lifetimes of humanity as long as time shall last." Paul combines references to both generations and ages in declaring his desire for God to receive "glory in the church and in Christ Jesus for all generations of the age of the ages." (Ephesians 3:21, my literal translation). As long as humans have lived, these concepts of generations and ages have measured our lifetimes. But Paul seems to imply in Ephesians that an eternal age awaits, which will include people from all the ages—the age of the ages.

## Strauss-Howe Generational Theory

While many historians in the modern age have sought to understand the cyclical nature of the generations from age to age, the most detailed and comprehensive theory emerged in 1991 from the work of William Strauss and Neil Howe in *Generations: The History of America's Future, 1584 to 2069*.[39] In that book, they analyze some 400 years of American history to discern how generations cycle through the course of the ages. *The theory they proposed can offer a powerful lens for understanding our times, as well as for predicting the timing of the next awakening in America.*

Indeed, Strauss-Howe Generational Theory provides the backbone of the analysis and predictions contained here. Not everyone agrees with or accepts the theory, nor should they. *It is good and healthy to take a critical view of all social science theories, and to read this book with some degree of skepticism, and perhaps, a greater degree of hope still.* No theory can perfectly account for reality, since words themselves only partially deliver the rich complexity of reality in a scaled-down framework that will fit between our ears.

Everything is more complicated that we can describe, and that makes theory incredibly important. Without theory, we cannot understand the world at all. Sometimes people will see theoretical knowledge as impractical, but they fail to understand that theory makes all action possible! All perception (sight, sound, smell, touch, taste) gets filtered through theory before we can act on it. Some people think curry smells unappealing. Some people think it tastes great. But people who think it smells bad usually never find out that it is delicious. Their theory about curry cancels out their willingness to try it.

Many historians reject Strauss-Howe Generational Theory for various reasons, especially its unfalsifiability, that is, its proponents cannot prove or disprove it by empirical testing. The data of history bear multiple interpretations. Further, because we can have no perfect record of all history, and since we cannot reliably predict the future, we cannot make absolute claims about the meaning of the past or the shape of the future.

We can stipulate up front that Generational Theory does not explain everything about history or predict the events of the future perfectly. But it can provide a framework for looking at history that can orient us powerfully in projecting the future. Our inability to predict the details of the future should not keep us from planning for it along the lines we can discern at the present. Those who do not plan for the future can have no hope for it, but the application of Generational Theory offers a highly plausible expectation for the future that should give hope to every living generation of Christians.

This book will not seek to present all the details of Generational Theory, nor even provide a richly footnoted summary of the work of Strauss and Howe. People who want to delve more deeply into the theory can read *Generations: The History of America's Future* to see how the authors interpret 400 years of American history. People who read the follow-up book from 1997, *The Fourth Turning: An American Prophecy,* can compare and evaluate the predictions of the theory with the actual events of the period of crisis we have lived through in the past couple of decades. *The Fourth Turning is Here: What the Seasons of History Tell us About How and When This Crisis Will End,* a recent (2023) follow-up book by Neil Howe, written after the death of Strauss, provides the most advanced presentation of the theory and its predictions for the second half of the 2020s and beyond.

Many readers will find Generational Theory compelling, but they will get only a brief and breezy summary here that leaves out a great deal of the elegance and rich specificity of the theory as its authors developed it. They should read the original books for greater insight. The purpose here seeks only to explore the implications of

Strauss and Howe's theory for Christian revival, the next Awakening, and how the Church should prepare itself for the years ahead.

**A Brief and Breezy Summary**

As a breezy interpretation and summary of the theory, generations and *saecula* (ages) offer the key elements of analysis. Generations have occurred every 20 years or so since the dawn of humanity. Every generation differs from the one that preceded it, in part because each generation experiences the events of history from different vantage points. Children experienced World War II in one way, young adults in another, middle-aged parents endured it differently, and elders and grandparents in other ways.

Each generation has a different level of experience and maturity as it processes life at different times. One who experienced the moon landing of 1969 as a child (whether in rapt fascination or forced attention) might have aspired to become an astronaut after growing up, while an elderly person would have processed it differently. Many things affect the way people engage with the world over the course of their lives, but they generally do it as members of a generation.

A lifetime usually includes experience of four simultaneous generational groups. A child in world history has typically experienced parents between the ages of 20 and 50, grandparents between the ages of 40 and 70, and great-grandparents between the ages of 70 and 100 —differing according to marital ages and their ages of first childbirth. As a person moves from one season of life to the next, a new generation emerges to replace the oldest one as it dies away. Psalm 90 and Ecclesiastes 1 described it all pretty well. Life has always worked that way.

Generational theory adds a powerful interpretive element to the natural progression of the generations. Similar to the way nature organizes an annual set of seasons— spring, summer, autumn, and winter—societies experience a cyclical repetition over the course of what we might call "generational seasons." Strauss and Howe call the first season a "High," characterized by an economic boom and societal success that lasts for about 20 years.

A High corresponds to springtime. During such a season, the adolescents and young adults experience a certain disillusionment with money and success and begin to yearn for deeper values —for spiritual prosperity. (Everyone considers money "the answer" until they get some, and their children tend to conclude that money does not provide the answer.) As a result, their transition to adulthood tends to bring about an "Awakening"—a summery season in which the society as a whole takes time off to pursue spiritual things. Religious and spiritual institutions as well as secular spiritualities experience growth and widespread attention for about 20 years, until the next generation of children comes to adulthood.

The children of an Awakening—much to their parents' chagrin—have cut their teeth on the pews and essentially know how the sausage is made. They tend to show more skepticism and even cynicism about religion and spirituality, and indeed, about institutions themselves. As they become adults, the society begins a season of "Unraveling," corresponding to autumn. Moral clarities become muddier. The economic boom of the High moves further into the background, as does the spiritual intensity of the Awakening, and society begins a process of decadence and the losing of community. Hopes do not run as high as they once did. Disillusion sets in over a period of twenty years.

In the fourth stage, society hits the wall in a wintry period of Crisis. Economic recessions and depressions set in, major wars break out, natural disasters carry a heavier impact. Institutions break up and close down. Governments get more involved with (and interfere with) the daily lives of citizens. As the crisis comes to an end and society resolves the issues produced by the Crisis, a new cycle begins again with a new High and a rebirth of prosperity and hope and community and institutional life.

Strauss and Howe beautifully illustrate the four cycles of a *saeculum* (age) through an analysis of the entirety of America's history. They do not suggest that the seasons/cycles work like a clock, and all kinds of historical disruptions can interfere with their rhythm. Sometimes, when whole societies disappear or experience an extended period of crisis, their cycles come to an end. America, however, has experienced a remarkable regularity of cycles over the years of its history. **God obviously does not have to follow Generational Theory in determining the affairs of humanity nor in responding to them, even if the theory actually describes God's normal way of dealing with societies.** Indeed, one of the critiques that historians have brought to the theory objects to its determinism. Christian theologians, like secular historians and philosophers and physicists have spent considerable effort trying to explain the relationship between determinism/ predestination and free will without solving the mystery, and we need not attempt to do so here.

The next chapter considers American history along these same lines of analysis in order to project what the next forty years may look like. Those who long for revival will find great hope in the years ahead.

# CHAPTER 4

# THE CYCLES OF AMERICAN HISTORY

Consider American history over the past couple of centuries through the categories of Strauss and Howe.  In 1801, the **Second Great Awakening** began with the Cane Ridge Revival at a Presbyterian camp meeting in Kentucky, which drew crowds of up to 20,000 people.  Over the following decades, Baptist and Methodist preachers passionately conducted revivals and planted churches across the Midwestern and Southern frontiers as millions of Americans turned to Christian faith.  Considered the "most influential revival in American history" by the eminent church historian Mark Noll, it set the template for the highly religious country America would become.[40] Out of it also grew important reform movements such as the Abolitionist movement.

In 1828, following the Awakening, the **Unraveling** began with the election of Andrew Jackson, a military hero and rough man of the people. Jackson bears responsibility for the cruel treatment of Native Americans in the Indian Removal Act and the Trail of Tears (1830-1850), in which the military forced America's indigenous populations out of the southeastern states into Oklahoma, the new "Indian Territory." After Jackson, American politics produced a long string of mediocre leaders who failed to solve the nation's growing problems. The Panic of 1837 resulted in a long economic depression that lasted into the Crisis period of the mid-1840s, with multiple recessions through the 1850s.

In 1846, a period of **Crisis** began with the conquest of Mexican lands in the West by means of the Mexican American War (1846-1848). The years that followed featured the expansion of slavery and moral conflict that would lead to the Secession of the Southern states and the beginning of the Civil War—the greatest period of conflict and division in the history of the nation. Many people consider today's moral crisis the most severe in all American history, but it we can hardly imagine a worse moral climate than one in which brothers and close relatives fought against and killed each other over the issue of whether to continue enslaving other human beings.

As Generational Theory would predict, the United States entered a **High** after the end of the Civil War in 1865. The Presidency of Ulysses S. Grant saw incredible prosperity and the development of the American West with the completion of the Transcontinental Railroad in 1869. The rise of the "Robber Barons" began during those years of rapid economic expansion. Known as the Gilded Age, its wealth lingers on in the massive Victorian homes that still grace the downtown residential neighborhoods of America's towns and cities today.

After twenty years or so, an **Awakening** emerged, led by the Holiness Movement—both Wesleyan and Keswickian branches. Evangelists and teachers like D. L. Moody, A. T. Pierson, A. J. Gordon, C. I. Scofield, A. B. Simpson, C. H. Spurgeon (and just about anyone else with two initials and a Bible) led remarkable revivals, enjoyed enormous followings, and founded new denominations. Perhaps the greatest fruit of this fourth American Awakening was the birth of the Student Volunteer Movement, founded in 1886, which resulted in over 20,000 Americans  responding to a call to foreign missionary service. (Prior to 1870, the United States had only produced about 2,000 missionaries in 200 years.)

Those missionaries had an enormous effect in evangelizing the world over the course of their lifetimes and over the succeeding generations, contributing to the greatest period of church growth in history up to that time. Strauss and Howe refer to the fourth Awakening as the "Missionary Awakening," which I would call the Missionary/Pentecostal Awakening because of the rising interest in Baptism in the Holy Spirit after 1870 that gave rise to the virtually simultaneous birth of Pentecostalism around the world. But the dawn of Pentecostalism and its worldwide dispersion through the Azusa Street Revival (1906-1908) gave the Awakening a long tail. As Pentecostalism took hold around the world, it had a major role in extending the continuous string of revivals that came in the wake of the Awakening in America and overseas over the following 100 years.

The fourth Awakening continues to have an effect through the movements it birthed, but its hold on America began to yield to an **Unraveling** around 1908 as Teddy Roosevelt left office (in fulfillment of an unwise promise not to seek re-election) and then worked to undermine his hand-picked successor, William Howard Taft. The presidency of Woodrow Wilson took America into World War I, following by the scandalous administration of Warren Harding, who died in office. The Roaring 20s with their signature "Flappers" and declining moral standards, the rise of Prohibition and the mobsters who infested America's cities, and a runaway stock market that ended on Black Friday with the stock market crash of 1929, sent America fully into a new **Crisis** cycle.

The **Crisis** of 1929-1945 was a doozy with the Great Depression, unemployment rates as high as 25%, the massive expansion of government under Franklin Roosevelt and the adoption of socialistic nanny-state programs, and eventually, America's entry into 1945. The entire world faced the gravest crisis in human history with Hitler's effort to establish the Third Reich, Japan's efforts to take over the Asia-Pacific region, the Holocaust, the death of millions due to the War, and the nuclear bombing of Japan.

Out of great crisis, however, a great **High** emerged. American leadership of the world after the Bretton Woods conference that set up the Post-War World Economic Order resulted in spectacular economic growth with the rebuilding of Germany and Japan and an era known as The Golden Age of Capitalism. Colonized nations of the world gained their independence and attracted massive economic investment. The Civil Rights Movement transformed American racial relations, and the Space Race resulted in the Apollo moon landings as advances in computer science set up a new age of technological development. The Post World War II Economic Boom was the largest in history up to that time, serving a rapidly increasing world population.

An **Awakening** began to emerge in the late 1960s, as young people began to hunger for spiritual experiences. In hard times, people think money will answer all their problems; in economic booms, they enjoy their newfound prosperity. But the generation of children they raise in plenty quickly figures out they need more than money to find fulfillment as human beings. The Baby Boom children of the Post World War II Era wanted more than money as they came to adulthood, rejecting the values of their parents and seeking to "find themselves." The Sexual Revolution that began after World War II led to young people looking for transcendence in sex and "free love," anti-war protest, psychedelic drugs, exotic and new religions, but the spiritual emptiness of these experiments led quickly to a religious turn.

By 1970, the Jesus Movement had burst on the scene and would go on to transform the lives of millions of Americans. Entwined with it came the Charismatic Movement, which emerged out of the Pentecostal Movement that had begun in the previous awakening and spread around the world. The Pentecostal-Charismatic emphasis on God's immediate presence through the indwelling and manifestations of the Holy Spirit influenced all Protestant denominations. The Roman Catholic Church also felt the impact of Pentecostalism in the Charismatic Renewal that began notably at Duquesne University in 1966 and quickly spread to the University of Notre Dame. As a result of this powerful echo of previous Awakenings came the greatest worldwide growth of Christianity in history, with almost four times as many Christians living in the world today than in 1910.[41]

Unfortunately, even the greatest of awakenings eventually declines, and the Televangelist scandals of 1987-89 served as powerful evidence that the Unraveling had begun. The final years of the Reagan administration were mired in the Iran-Contra Scandal and the emerging Savings and Loan failures. The one-term presidency of George H. W. Bush followed, spoiled by unkept promises of "no new taxes" as budget struggles brought fiscal conflict. The scandal-ridden Clinton administration came next with the Monica Lewinsky debacle and a subsequent impeachment trial, and the George W. Bush administration faced the false crisis of Y2K, the Dotcom Bust, the horrific terrorist attacks of September 11, 2001, and the beginnings of the Iraq and Afghanistan wars, lead to the beginning of a full-scale **Crisis** period by 2007.

The Global Financial Crisis of 2007-2008 brought the most severe economic reversal since the Great Depression and gave birth to the latest twenty-year cycle. In the following decades, the World would face not only economic challenge but also the COVID-19 pandemic, the Russian-Ukraine War, and the barbarous massacre of Jews in Israel by Hamas on October 6, 2023. The failure of younger leaders to emerge in America led to the gerontocratic rule of America's oldest presidents, Donald J. Trump and Joseph R. Biden. During their administrations, the country faced the most serious political polarization since the Civil War.

When and how will the Crisis Period end? Neil Howe expects that "America will exit winter and enter Spring in the early or mid-2030s."[42] The Hungarian-American futurologist and geopolitical consultant George Friedman predicted, in his 2020 book *The Storm Before the Calm: America's Discord, the Coming Crisis of the 2020s, and the Triumph Beyond,* that America would emerge from this period of crisis in the late 2020s.[43] Based on other cyclical theories of history, he reckons that America's "eighty-year institutional cycle" and its "fifty-year socio-economic cycle" will converge in the late 2020s, bringing societal upheaval, potential conflict, and a resolution of the polarization and culture wars we experienced in the recent past. As Friedman predicted in his previous 2009 book, *The Next 100 Years: A Forecast for the 21$^{st}$ Century,* he once again projected that America will return to a position of strength, continued wealth, and global power.[44]

The interpretation of cyclical history in the United States made me wonder whether Biblical history demonstrated a similar pattern. Those who find that question interesting can find an analysis of the history of the Kingdom of Judah (beginning with Saul) in Appendix 1.

Americans have very good reasons to trust Friedman's predictions about their future, not the least of which depends on the nature of God, who responds to the prayers of God's people and will either bless us with the Return of Christ in the next 20 years or another Awakening that will give us spiritual fuel for the years ahead. Generational Theory predicts a societal high sometime during the next 20 to 25 years, and America still enjoys the world's best economy due to the massive size of our internal market, the incredible richness of our agricultural lands, and the enduring attractiveness of our country to the world's brightest and most ambitious immigrants —especially from those countries that profile as our gravest threats. It's hard to defeat a nation (America) when all your best citizens want to immigrate to that country and become, well, Americans.

Nevertheless, obstacles stand in the way of the next High. The "Buffett Indicator," which compares the total value of U.S. stocks to the Gross Domestic Product, sees equities as "extremely overvalued."[45] A major stock market crash could happen at any time, creating massive losses for investors and hard times for a while, but also eventually setting up a more solid foundation for economic growth. We also face a global sovereign debt crisis, which the secretary-general of the United Nations has called one of "the biggest threats to global peace."[46]

America has the world's largest sovereign debt ever, owing tens of trillions of dollars to itself and global investors. We also have a stubborn inflation rate and continuing high interest rates that show little signs of abating. The International Monetary Fund recently warned the United States that "U.S. government budget deficits and an escalating debt load pose "a growing risk" to the global economy" despite its recognition that America has had "an otherwise stellar economic performance" since the end of the pandemic."[47]

We face real vulnerability to hyperinflation as the BRICS nations (Brazil, Russia, India, China, and South Africa) resent our long winning streak and plot constantly to end the dominance of the dollar.[48] The All-Volunteer military faces a severe recruiting crisis, and we constantly hear that America has grown tired of serving as the World's Policeman.[49] That role primarily consists in the security America's Navy provides for the current globalized economic system in protecting the sea lanes and ensuring the stability of global supply chains.

Geopolitical strategist Peter Zeihan predicts, in his 2022 book *The End of the World is Just the Beginning: Mapping the Collapse of Globalization*, that globalization will fail soon precisely because America has lost interest in keeping it going and will back away from its comprehensive patrolling of the seas. He believes that the coming end of globalization and the collapse of the world population will result in famine and war around the world, which the United States will not police or resolve. Still, he believes that America will rebuild its manufacturing sector and provide for its own needs while letting the world go its own way.

Zeihan's prediction of the end of globalization may fail, but he rightly judges that America will find a way to prosper in the future. That future prosperity probably lies just a few years away, and the results of the 2024 presidential election will shape the following four years in unpredictable ways. But whoever serves as America's next president will have an incredible opportunity to lead an end to the culture wars (forming an America that agrees to live and let live on a variety of moral issues that have divided us recently and for decades past). The next president (or the following one) will likely face a worldwide sovereign debt crisis (that is, debt held by governments) and possibly even a hyperinflationary crisis.

We can probably assume that government economists have already "war-gamed" how they would sanitize America's debt and replace the current dollar. If the relatively recent experience of currency meltdowns in Ecuador and El Salvador offers any guide, the "Death of the Dollar," as prophecy teacher Willard Cantelon famously predicted, would probably lead to a couple of years of austerity. An incredible economic boom would follow, after the world realizes that all the buildings and products of debt financing still stand. Everyone would still need goods and services, and every single person in the world would have grown sick of the austerity and would feel ready to rumble economically.

The next 25 years will give us a wild ride! And when it's over, the finest hour of the American church could very well have arrived. We have a couple of decades to plan for it and build it. While the shape of the future can always surprise us, and the generational cycle could suffer delays or even come to an end, the framework provided by Generational Theory probably presents the most likely scenario for the future. It's always possible that America may run out of steam in the years ahead, as every other great society in history has. Civil War could bring America as we know it to an end, as some predict. Jesus could return at any time to bring the end of the age. But the most likely immediate future calls for a resolution of our current malaise, a period of societal High, and the Sixth Great Awakening in due time. So, the next chapter will look further into generational theory to suggest what the next generations of spiritual leaders will look like.

| Cycles of American History (1620-2065) | | |
|---|---|---|
| Cycle | Dates | Events |
| Awakening | 1621–1649 | The Puritan Awakening (#1). Although historians coined the phrase "First Great Awakening" to refer to a later event, this event was the first spiritual awakening in American history. |
| Unraveling | 1649–1675 | Restoration of the Stewart family to the throne |
| Crisis | 1675–1704 | The "Glorious Revolution," dynastic change |
| High | 1704–1727 | The English Enlightenment |
| Awakening | 1727-1746 | The First Great Awakening (#2) |
| Unraveling | 1746-1773 | French and Indian War |
| Crisis | 1773-1789 | The Revolutionary War and the Articles of Confederation |
| High | 1789-1804 | economic growth in the new Republic |
| Awakeni | 1801-1824 | The Second Great |

| ng | | Awakening, Cane Ridge, Abolitionism (#3) |
|---|---|---|
| Unraveling | 1824-1845 | Trail of Tears, Panic of 1837, economic depression |
| Crisis | 1845-1865 | Mexican War, Recessions, Civil War |
| High | 1865-1886 | U.S. Grant years, westward expansion, railroads |
| Awakening | 1886-1908 | Holiness Movement, Student Volunteer Movement, Pentecostalism (#4) |
| Unraveling | 1908-1929 | World War I, The Roaring 20s, Prohibition and the Mobs |
| Crisis | 1929-1946 | Great Depression and World War II |
| High | 1946-1968 | The Post-World War II Boom and Post-Colonial Global Development |
| Awakening | 1968-1986 | The Jesus movement and the Charismatic Movement (#5) |
| Unraveling | 1987-2007 | Televangelist Scandals, Monica Lewinsky, Y2K, Dotcom Bust, 9/11 attacks |

| Crisis | 2007-2028 | Global Financial Crisis, Iraq and Afghanistan Wars, COVID-19 pandemic, Trump and Biden presidencies, Russia-Ukraine War, Gaza War, Monetary/Sovereign Debt crisis |
| --- | --- | --- |
| High | 2028—2045 | Success |
| Awakening | 2045-2065 | The Sixth Great Awakening[50] |

# CHAPTER 5

# CURRENT GENERATIONS AND THE NEXT AWAKENING

Generational Theory suggests that generations undergo a profound shaping through the circumstances they experience (events such as 9/11 or the assassinations of John and Robert Kennedy and Martin Luther King, Jr. or Black Friday, the stock market crash in 1929). But the period of life in which they experience societal crises also shapes them. It would be a profound error for anyone to assume that all members of a generation think and act the same way. To use Generational Theory in such as way as to impose a deterministic character on every member of a generation would constitute a very foolish approach. Each person responds individually to the events and challenges of his or her time and develops a unique personality and character. Nevertheless, members of a generation do seem to share common characteristics, at least in the aggregate, according to their shared experiences of the events of their time.

Just as Strauss and Howe propose four cycles for each age or *saeculum (High, Awakening, Unraveling, and Crisis)*, they describe four generational "archetypes" that define each generation of young adults: artist, prophet, nomad, and hero. **Artist generations** face Crisis as children, when they learn self-sacrifice for the good of their families and communities. They become young adults during a High as conformists, having learned resignation during the crisis. They tend toward a process orientation rather than idealism. In their 40s and 50s they experience an Awakening, to which they respond with a certain coolness and skepticism. In their old age they rule wisely. **Prophet** generations define themselves during an Awakening and tend to evangelize for their cause and for an exalted spiritual life. Positive and optimistic, having grown up in prosperity, they successfully govern during a crisis.

**Nomad generations** find definition during a decline and tend toward alienation and suspicion of institutions. They begin life during an Awakening, to which they react suspiciously during adolescence or young adulthood. They tend to feel unprotected and ignored by their parents. In their youth they become pragmatic rather than idealistic and alienated from social institutions such as the church. In their old age, they govern with pragmatism. And finally, **Hero** generations grow up during an Unraveling and suffer overprotection as children. When they become young adults, they experience a Crisis, during which they tend to prefer to work in teams and with optimism. They reach their prime during a High and lead the Society to prosperity by renewing social institutions such as the church.

Strauss and Howe point out that the prophet and hero generations have a **dominant** character, while the nomadic and artist generations take a **recessive** position—alternating according to the challenges that define them as a generation. Illustrating the different generational types, the **Hero** generation that fought World War II and presided over the Golden Age of Capitalism has been called "The **Greatest Generation**." They successfully weathered a Crisis in their 20s and 30s, oversaw a time of great prosperity during their 40s and 50s, and ruled in the midst of an

Awakening during their old age. Experiencing problems during one's years of better health and strength offers great benefit! No one wants to face crisis in the senior years. The heroic performance of the Greatest Generation in their youth made them a dominant generation.

The **Artist** generation that followed the Greatest Generation emerged between 1925 and 1942 and experienced the Great Depression and World War II Crisis as children. Called the **"Silent Generation,"** they enjoyed the post-war economic boom during their youth (avoiding the need to step up as heroes) and came to the Jesus-Movement Awakening as parents during their 40s and 50s—greeting it with a conservative and suspicious attitude. They experienced old age in a period of decline. As a recessive generation, they were destined not to stand out.

They generally performed poorly in the line of presidential succession. Jimmy Carter (born in 1924 and attending college instead of fighting in World War II) saw his presidency suffer a resounding national rejection as the nation turned back to the Greatest Generation in the election of Ronald Reagan instead of trusting the rising generation of leaders. George H. W. Bush, born the same year as Jimmy Carter, fought in World War II and shared more of the characteristics of the Greatest Generation, although his presidency also suffered rejection as the country turned to the young Bill Clinton instead of letting another member of the Artist generation govern.

As mentioned above, many members of the Silent Generation received the Jesus Movement and the Charismatic Movement with suspicion and caution and even rejection, but some leaders—especially Pentecostal Pastors—took up the challenge of leadership well. Pastor Chuck Smith (born 1927), depicted in the movie "Jesus Revolution," overcame his initial skepticism toward the Jesus Movement and provided stellar leadership in channeling the movement into institutional form in the Calvary Chapel churches.[51] Other Pentecostal churches such as the Assemblies of God and myriad independent churches experienced massive growth.

Many Silent Generation pastors wrapped their arms around the new believers, who flooded into their churches full of incredible spiritual zeal and passion, with their hippie clothes, new musical styles, and revolutionary spirit. Older pastors reinterpreted the traditions of Christian spirituality for young people and passed on the historic Christian doctrinal structures and helped young people temper their enthusiasms with wisdom and tradition. In the next generation, the Artist Generation (Gen Z), together with the older Millennial Generation, will have a tremendous opportunity to do the same for the yet-unborn generation that will experience the Awakening as teenagers and young adults.

**Baby Boomers and Gen X**

Next came a **Prophet** generation. The **Baby Boomers** (born **1943-1964**) experienced prosperity in their childhood High, the Awakening during their youth (which made them "prophets"), the Unraveling in their maturity, and the Crisis during their cycle of old age. Bill Clinton (who came to government at a young age and before his due time, eclipsing leaders from the previous generation) once complained in an informal conversation that he could not achieve greatness as president because he governed in a time of calm. But other members of his generation would hang around past their time to face the Crisis of recent years.

Early Boomers like Trump and Biden governed the country in their advanced old age because the next generation did not inspire confidence that they could rise to the challenge of leadership, being a recessive **Nomad** generation. Members of Gen X (born 1965-1981) experienced the Jesus Movement and the Charismatic Movement in their childhood and came to feel wary of religion. They saw a lot of hypocrisy and drama in the church (and in society at large) during their early years and were reluctant to embrace the religious experiences and societal memberships of their parents. When observers first began to recognize them in the 1990s, some observers predicted that they would not take their place of institutional leadership in large numbers and would get passed over for leadership in favor of the next generation. That prediction has proved generally true.[52] Only time will tell whether the Millennial generation will usurp the turn of Gen X American politicians.

Robert Putnam's 2000 book, *Bowling Alone: The Collapse and Revival of American Community* described the loss of social capital in America as people increasingly stopped participating in voluntary organizations and organized group activities.[53] Gen X certainly does not bear the blame for that trend, but it did little to restore America's social institutions. Members of Gen X defined themselves during the Unraveling and suffered the Crisis with a distinct stoicism. They left the church in large numbers, as did the generations that succeeded them, and many of them raised their children with little or no religious training, setting up 'the rise of the Nones."

**The Millennials**

Generational theorists hailed the next generation as a **Hero** generation, calling them the **Millennials** (born 1982-2005). They entered the world during the Unraveling and defined themselves during the Crisis, fighting in Iraq and Afghanistan, creating social media and cryptocurrencies, and leading in a time of unprecedented technological advance. They will figure as economic heroes during the coming boom, technological pioneers who will change the world and breathe new life into institutions like the church. They currently plant most new churches, and they will found many more in the coming years of prosperity.

The Millennials will resemble the Greatest Generation and will have a strong impact during the next Awakening in their 50s and 60s— a phenomenon they will have never experienced before but seem likely to embrace. They heard from the parents and grandparents about the glories of the Jesus Movement and saw the Jesus Revolution movie, and Christian leaders among them long to see revival in the churches and an Awakening in society. The young people who lead the Sixth Great Awakening will see them as reliable allies and look to them for guidance. Society as a whole will look to them for an extended period of governance.

**Gen Z**

The current generation of young people have been labeled as Gen Z (born 2006-present), although the generic label may yield to something more descriptive in the future as their defining moment crystallizes. Born during the current Crisis and strongly affected by the COVID-19 pandemic and society's failed response to it, the members of Gen Z will find definition in the coming High. Some observers have called them the Zoomers because they suffered through so many Zoom meetings.

Generational Theory suggests they will

profile as a recessive **Artist** generation like the Silent Generation before them. Although some observers want to replace them prematurely with a so-called Alpha generation, only time will tell when the next generation emerges. The generations definitely have fuzzy borders, as people born toward the end of a generation can identify with the following one, even as people born at the beginning of a generation may look backward for identity.

Gen Z will come to definition during the upcoming High. They will look much like the generation before the Jesus Movement. They will experience the Sixth Great Awakening in their 30s and 40s, and they will show a little suspicion for what the next generation will promote. They will have a major role, however, in passing on 2,000 years of Christian tradition and wisdom to the next generation, just as Silent Generation pastors like Chuck Smith taught the Jesus People who came to his church in the early 1970s and afterward. **If the Church can train a generation of revival-shaped, faithful Gen Z Christians to support the youth of the following generation, they will serve as powerful allies and effective leaders of the next Awakening.**

**The Characteristics of Gen Z**

Many books and articles offer insights into the current generation of young people,[54] and they clearly face a set of challenges unlike those of any generation before them. The effect of the COVID-19 pandemic and the aggressive reaction to it by government has scarred them, although they will heal from it as they come to maturity. Still, more trauma may wait in store over the middle and late years of the 2020s. **In any case, Gen Z has incredible potential for making a very significant contribution to the Sixth Great Awakening.** Whatever people may say about this generation in the aggregate, individual members of this generation will rise to the occasion of leadership in the next great awakening.

Gen X members mocked the Millennial generation as "babies on board" because of the cutesy signs their proud parents hung in the back windows of their cars.[55] Overprotected by their adoring parents, the Millennials only made Gen X members feel more like neglected "latch-key kids."[56] In contrast to the Millennials, the recessive Gen Z feels *under protected* by their nevertheless *overprotective* parents and teachers and other adults.[57] Social psychologist Jonathan Haidt has called them, "The Anxious Generation" because of the epidemic of anxiety (134% increase in diagnoses since 2010), depression (106% increase since 2010) and related mental illnesses such as ADHD, Bipolar Disorder, schizophrenia, self-harm, gender dysphoria, and substance abuse suffered among this generation.[58]

Famous for complaining that they do not feel safe, as taught to feel by their teachers at public and progressive private schools, Gen Z school children saw many of their teachers declare that they felt unsafe around them during the pandemic, essentially telling them to go home and go to their rooms, that they were "on their own" to study online. Although many heroic teachers did their best to mitigate the harm, Gen Z students lost two or more years of learning,[59] and now, more and more of them opt out of higher education.[60] Only 13% feel prepared to make a decision about their future.[61]

Having been entertained, educated, and baby-sat by the internet and social media, members of Gen Z grew up as digital natives. They spend a LOT of time online, up to 60 hours per week.[62] Many of them lack durable attention spans and struggle to process complex ideas or synthetic information that comes from various sources.[63] They criticize themselves as "lacking motivation."[64] They don't feel safe and are always look for security. They don't like big crowds.

Like every generation past, they struggle to "find themselves," but they suffer the most serious identity crisis ever recorded, with unprecedented numbers of them identifying as homosexual or bisexual or asexual or transgender or any of 58 other gender identities offered as choices on Facebook.[65] They demonstrate greater caution in sexual experimentation, having less sex than any generation in recent memory.[66] They use

20% less alcohol than the general population, but suffer from other substance abuse problems.[67] As activists, they want to advocate for great causes, but they feel skeptical about the reality of change.[68] Members of Gen Z generally distrust institutions but pay close attention to "influencers," especially through digital media like Instagram and TikTok.[69]

As the least religious generation since the Revolutionary War, they came of age during a time known as The Dechurching of America.[70] Nevertheless, 25% of Gen Z adults report attending services weekly.[71] This compares to 28% of the total adult population. While overall religious participation rate for Gen Z shows a dramatic drop in nominal association with Christianity, they show percentages of high involvement that should encourage hope. **These highly committed Gen Z Christians will provide a great resource of faith for their generation in the future, as well as for the next generation.**

If on the one hand, Gen Z tends to evidence a short attention span, having become avid consumers of short-form Tik Tok videos, on the other hand its members have also contributed to the popularity of long-form interviews by intellectuals like Joe Rogan and Jordan Peterson (proving they can pay attention when their interest engages a topic).[72] Reading scores among students have dropped significantly since the Pandemic to the lowest level in decades.[73] According to Atlantic reporter Xochitl Gonzales, "Plummeting reading comprehension is a national problem, but it's particularly acute in New York City. Half of its third to eighth graders—and 60 percent of those who are Black and Latino—cannot read at grade level."[74]

If many Gen Z members cannot or do not read books, the ones who do read take such an avid approach to it that they have created a boom in book sales in recent years. According to Book Riot:

Gen Z helped contribute to another great year in book sales in 2022. Although sales were down from a record strong year in 2021 by 6.5%, Publishers Weekly reported a very respectable 788.7 million books sold in 2022. Trade paperbacks actually sold more in 2022 than usual (comprising 60% of sales), and hardcover sales declined by 3%. Despite 67% of Gen Zers surveyed reading on their phones, those paperback sales are, in large part, due to Gen Z readers.[75]

It is foolish to judge any generation of human beings as somehow defective, or to judge its strongest members on the basis of its weakest. Members of Gen X, the Millennials, and Gen Z have proven that they can rise to great heights, just as some members of previous generations proved they could descend to unspeakable lows. We have no valid reason to think that Gen Z has a lower intelligence potential than previous generations or a lower sense of conscience than previous generations, and in their young adulthood, they will experience a societal High that will motivate them to financial responsibility and personal industriousness. *Maturity looks good on everyone, and like every other generation, experience will benefit Gen Z.*

As Gen Z matures, they may get married and have children later than previous generations, but most of them will eventually settle down. Most importantly, Christians in Gen Z demonstrate a remarkable hunger for God and desire for revival. While less of them have chosen to study for church ministry,[76] those who do answer the call to ministry have unprecedented access to biblical and theological education due to the resources of the Internet and increasingly, artificial Intelligence. Their turn to rise to the spiritual challenge of an Awakening will come, and they will answer it.

The spiritual formation of Gen Z represents the greatest challenge and opportunity faced by today's Church, whether delivered in local congregations or parachurch organizations or educational institutions or other modalities. *Northwest University, where I serve as president, sees its whole mission as training leaders for the next Great Awakening, and so should every other Christian educational institution in America.*

The students we educate in our classrooms today and tomorrow will carry the accumulated knowledge of Scripture, the theological reflections, the practical Christian wisdom, the structural lessons, the missional strategies, and the corporate memories of 2,000 years of Church history. Obviously, they won't have all the details in their minds, but they will have unparalleled access to learning opportunities on the Internet to feed into the structural categories they gain in formal and informal educational settings.

And then there's one more thing, which the next chapter will explore. In the 20 years preceding the next Awakening in America, churches will experience significant revival. Revivals always motivate Christians to study and to receive teaching, and as revival comes to prepare the church for harvesting the next Awakening, Gen Z Christians will develop a passion for learning.

# CHAPTER 6

# THE EVE OF AN AWAKENING

What should we expect in the years between 2025 and 2050? Obviously, the details of the future have proven impossible to predict with any confidence, but the predictions of the future that I saw as a child have pretty faithfully come true. I often marvel at the "Picture Phone" I carry in my pocket. Smart phones vastly exceeded the expectations given to schoolkids in the early 1970s. Dick Tracy would have killed for an Apple Watch.

Far from a foolhardy thing, predicting the future can have a huge role in shaping what happens, since people tend to get what they work for and achieve what they have faith for. Consider these possible futures for the United States in the next 25 years:

- Jesus could come, ushering in the end of the world as we know it and the beginning of "the Age to Come," as Luke 18 refers to the time of eternity. Christians have varying expectations about the *ordo finis*, ranging from immediate paradise to a seven-year Great Tribulation. When people ask me if I think we're in the Great Tribulation, I always answer, "We can only hope so." Whatever it takes to get to "Kingdom Come," I'm up for it.
- An Awakening could happen on time or **earlier than expected** and spread around the world, serving as the final Harvest of Souls before the Second Coming of Christ.
- Instead of a new High cycle followed by an Awakening, we could see the generational cycle come to an end in America. Imagine a serious and sustained monetary crisis, world war, nuclear holocaust, civil war, or other unthinkable outcomes. Those kinds of events would disturb and perhaps even put an end to the natural generational cycle, and then anything can happen except something good.

- We will see the current Crisis cycle finish sometime between 2025 and 2030, giving way to a High in which the United States enters a new economic boom and finds a new societal consensus on the culture war issues that have divided the country since about 1971.

As the title of this book declares, I believe we will see the Sixth Great Awakening occur in America sometime in the next 25 years. Generational cycles can last for periods shorter or longer than 20 years, as the timing can vary unpredictably.

**The Twenty Years Before the Last Awakening**

If so, looking at the twenty years before 1968 would seem to recommend the best way of predicting what the next two decades (2025-2045) will look like. According to Tobin Grant of Religious News Service,

"Coming out of World War II, America was not very religious. The war had put a halt on many of the things that increase religiosity, particularly marriage and procreation. Churches, just like other organizations, were slowed by drain on resources and volunteers during the war.[77]

That general description matches the present time, which Davis, Graham, and Burge have called The Great Dechurching of America.[78]

**Christian Vitality Today**

One way to judge Christian vitality in

America measures church membership. As According to the Gallup Organization, which has tracked church membership since 1939, America has suffered a dramatic drop since the late 1990s.[79] In 1939, 73% of Americans reported membership in a church, synagogue, or mosque, and that remained relatively steady until 2000, when it stood at 70%. But the percentage of American who hold membership in a religious congregation dropped steadily over two decades to reach 47% in 2020, a total drop of about 36%.

Another measure of vitality considers weekly attendance at worship. Gallup gauges attendance across various religions by asking, "Did you, yourself, happen to attend church, synagogue, mosque, or temple in the last seven days or not?". The reports of attendance across the major religions held more or less steady around 40% for about seventy years since 1939 except for a sharp increase to 59% in the late 1950s, which may largely result from exaggerated claims of church attendance during the strongly pro-Christian Eisenhower administration.[80] (Observers have noted that American houses of worship would not have had sufficient space in the pews to accommodate 59% of the population on a weekly basis, but Americans probably did not want to admit to pollsters that they did not attend services weekly). But despite remarkable consistency in the reports of weekly attendance at worship from 1939 until 2010, attendance has declined significantly in recent years, with the Gallup Organization reporting:

"Three in 10 Americans say they attend religious services every week (21%) or almost every week (9%), while 11% report attending about once a month and 56% seldom (25%) or never (31%) attend . . . Two decades ago, an average of 42% of U.S. adults attended religious services every week or nearly every week."[81]

But attendance at worship services only represents one element of religious and moral decline in our time.

According to data scientists Esteban Ortiz-Ospina and Max Roser, "Since 1972, marriage rates in the US have fallen by almost 50% and are currently at the lowest point in recorded history."[82] As such facts would predict, fertility and childbirth have also declined to historically low rates.[83] The idea that religion increases during hard times does not consistently fit the pattern of American religious history. To the contrary, religion tends to increase during Highs and Awakenings rather than during Unravelings and Crises, although local revivals can happen in any season. (An example would be the revivals that occurred among both United States and Confederate troops during the Civil

War.)

**The Postwar Era in America**

After World War II, when a High season began, marriage rates soared as America roared out of the Great Depression. The Gross National Product of the United States grew from $200 million in 1940 to $300 million in 1950 and continued rising to $500 million by 1960 as millions of Americans joined the middle class.[84] With the growing economy and an increase in marriages, fertility soared, giving birth to the massive Baby Boom generation.

And churches grew. Young families formed and went back to church. The Evangelical Movement thrived among conservative churches. Parachurch institutions emerged, and Bible colleges and Christian liberal arts colleges caught fresh wind or rose up from nothing as the 1943 Servicemen's Readjustment Act, popularly known as "the GI Bill," provided funds to send World War II veterans to college. Youth for Christ (1944), the National Association of Evangelicals (1942), Christianity Today Magazine (1956), and a host of missionary sending agencies and campus ministries like Intervarsity (1941), Campus Crusade for Christ (1951),[85] and other agencies came into being to fuel the growth of Christianity between 1945 and 1965.

**The Ministry of Billy Graham**

Among those organizations, Youth for Christ would introduce to the world a sensational young evangelist named Billy Graham in 1944. The first Billy Graham Crusade was held on September 13–21, 1947 in Grand Rapids, Michigan, and attracted 6,000 people.[86] A couple of years later in 1949, Graham's ministry achieved international notoriety when media magnate William Randolph Hearst sent a telegram to his newspapers with a simple message, "Puff Graham."[87] Graham would preach to millions of people around the world in the ensuing decades, becoming a household name around the world and an advisor to all subsequent United States presidents for the rest of his life.

The early years of Graham's ministry did not occur during an Awakening as defined by Generational Theory, but that hardly means that his first twenty years of ministry lacked impact. According to Molly Worthen of The Nation, Graham's "radio (and later television) show Hour of Decision reached 20 million homes in the 1950s.[88] After his spectacular London Crusade in 1954, Graham was featured on the cover of Time Magazine—the leading and most respected news medium of the day.[89] Appearing on the cover of Time and being featured in the cover article signified recognition as the hottest newsmaker in the nation. The 1960s saw only continued growth in his ministry, and over the course of "his sixty years of full-time evangelism, 215 million people heard him preach in person, and another 2 billion tuned in to telecasts."[90]

## The Healing Revival

Billy Graham, however, was hardly lonesome on the evangelistic circuit during the 1950s. The healing campaigns of Oral Roberts, in contrast to Billy Graham's more rational approach to preaching, drew crowds of tens of thousands with their reports of signs, wonders, healings and miracles. Like Billy Graham, Roberts became a pioneer of televangelism, taking his popular ministry to success in radio in 1947 and television in 1954. In 1963, he founded Oral Roberts University in Tulsa, Oklahoma. Over the years, he organized and preached over 300 revival campaigns on six continents, personally laying hands on more than 2 million people to pray for their healing.[91]

But Roberts was only one of many evangelists in the 1950s who saw massive response to prayer for divine healing and spectacular reports of miraculous intervention from God. While Oral Roberts saw phenomenal results to his prayers for healing, William M. Branham's ministry preceded him, and the reports from his ministry set off the healing revivals of the late 1940s and 1950s.[92] Scores of evangelists led healing revivals, with ministries of varying sizes and extents, meeting in venues from open-air fields, small to large churches, circus-style tents, civic auditoriums, and stadiums. The signs and wonders produced in these meetings had an unquestionable impact on the rise of the Charismatic Movement of the 1960s and Seventies and throughout the subsequent Awakening. Among those evangelists of the 1950s and early Sixties figured Gordon Lindsay, T. L. Osborn, Jack Coe, the disgraced A.A. Allen, and perhaps the most famous, Kathryn Kuhlman, who gained fame in the 1950s and had a television program on CBS.

A movement originally called "The New Order of the Latter Rain" also broke out within Pentecostalism in connection with the healing revivals. Beginning in Saskatchewan, Canada in about 1948 in response to a healing crusade conducted by William Branham, the new movement would stress healings, miracles, signs, and wonders. The Latter Rain had a large effect on the emerging Charismatic Movement and on revivalist Christianity to this day. While rejected by the Pentecostal denominations (not to mention mainstream Evangelicalism), large numbers of independent churches found inspiration and renewal through the Latter Rain's emphasis on revival and the power of God at work in the world today.

The movement had many extreme teachings like the emergence of "the manifest sons of God," through which some Christians would receive their glorified bodies and operate in full divine power here and now, and as a result faced rejection from the more sober and biblically-based historic Pentecostal churches. But other prominent doctrines of the Latter Rain found wide acceptance, including:

- direct revelation (personal prophecies, words of knowledge or wisdom)
- the gifts of the Spirit, received through the laying on of hands
- demonization of Christians requiring deliverance
- the restoration of the five-fold ministry of Ephesians 4:11, especially apostles and prophets
- divine healing through the laying on of hands
- praise and worship to usher in God's presence
- full access to all ministry roles for women
- the breakdown of denominational lines and unity in the Church.[93]

Anyone familiar with the Charismatic Movement can easily see how many of the Latter Rain emphases found long-term purchase in the churches.

**Revival from the Top**

Lest anyone think that revival only occurred among the "sawdust trail" crowd of poor people who met in circus tents or small country churches —and God certainly blessed them for their spiritual hunger, especially in my family—the whole nation saw a remarkable surge in religion during the 1950s. Revival swept the country from the bottom up, but also from the top down. The emerging Charismatic or "neo-Pentecostal" movement began to affect Mainline Protestant churches, which tended to serve the middle, professional, and upper classes, in the 1950s after South African Pentecostal leader David DuPlessis began to attend meetings of the World Council of Churches in 1954.[94]

Forming friendships with academic leaders like President John McKay of Princeton Theological Seminary and President Henry P. Van Dusen of New York's prestigious Union Theological Seminary, as well as other important denominational leaders, he not only formed strong ecumenical relationships but also took advantage of every opportunity to share his Pentecostal belief in the ongoing ministry of the Holy Spirit. Du Plessis prayed with many Mainline Protestant leaders to receive the Baptism in the Holy Spirit—as Pentecostals described the particular ecstatic spiritual experience that was the hallmark of the Charismatic Movement.[95] In 1960, the fledgling Charismatic Movement came to the attention of the nation when Episcopal priest Dennis J. Bennett announced from the pulpit of his large church in Van Nuys, California that he had been baptized in the Holy Spirit and had spoken in tongues. Promptly fired by the church, his *story soon* appeared in feature articles in the two leading news magazines,

Newsweek and Time—further spreading the new spiritual movement.[96]

## Communism and Dwight D. Eisenhower

America's greatest threat during the 1950's came from Communists at home and abroad who sought to transform the nation along Marxist lines. The growing popularity of evangelist Billy Graham as a strong defender of the American system of government and economics, among other things, led newly elected President Dwight D. Eisenhower to champion Protestant Christianity as a bulwark against Communism.[97] In a speech given after his election in 1952, Eisenhower said:

> It seems to me that if we are going to win this fight we have got to go back to the very fundamentals of all things. And one of them is that we are a religious people. Even those among us who are, in my opinion, so silly as to doubt the existence of an Almighty, are still members of a religious civilization, because the Founding Fathers said it was a religious concept they were trying to translate into the political world. Now, I don't mean to come before you and be evangelical in my approach, but what I do say is this: There, it seems to me, is the basic doctrine to which we must always cling.[98]

Eisenhower would soon make a more total commitment to his strategy for saving

America from Communism.

Although Eisenhower's parents had raised him among Mennonite Brethren and Jehovah's Witnesses, he had never been baptized. On February 1, 1953, Ten days after his inauguration, Eisenhower submitted himself to baptism at National Presbyterian Church under Rev. Edward Elson—the only U.S. President ever baptized in office. The country followed suit. **Church membership rose from 49 percent of Americans in 1940 to 69 percent in 1960—the highest percentage of church membership ever achieved in American history.**[99]

Eisenhower not only joined the Presbyterian church, but he also used his office frequently to promote Christian faith. At his inauguration, he began his speech with a prayer. Following the lead of Abraham Vereide, who had led city-wide prayer breakfasts in Seattle and a statewide Governor's Prayer Breakfast in Washington State, Eisenhower attended the National Prayer Breakfast in 1953 along with Billy Graham. The event still draws leaders of both political parties together annually for a public prayer meeting and routinely receives strong press attention and serves as a barometer of the nation's spiritual state. In 1954, Eisenhower succeeded in having Congress establish "In God We Trust" as the official motto of the United States, placing it on American paper currency to declare that God, and not money, would remain the anchor of our faith.

**Media Coverage of Theologians**

While Evangelical Protestantism began to enter its heyday during the 1950s, the historic Protestant churches had even greater favor with the media. *Time* Magazine featured the Anglican lay theologian C. S. Lewis on its cover in 1947. Responding to his book *Miracles: A Preliminary Investigation*, the magazine's editors were amazed that a leading academic would publicly affirm supernatural Christianity.[100]  Lewis became a household name among American Christians as his books sold by the millions and remain popular 80 years later.  Along with Billy Graham, *Time* also featured Protestant theologians from Union Theological Seminary in New York on its cover, namely Reinhold Niebuhr (1948)[101] and Paul Tillich (1959)[102].  Swiss theologian Karl Barth appeared on the cover of Time in 1962.[103]

Niebuhr, Tillich, and Barth were celebrated in the 1950s as "neo-orthodox" theologians, largely because their theology more or less rejected the radical skepticism of Nineteenth-Century liberal Protestantism in a return to the Bible as a major source of theological authority, without embracing the Evangelical view of scriptural infallibility.  Neither did these so-called neo-orthodox theologians necessarily accept the historic Christian doctrines asserted by the Fundamentalist Movement in Evangelical

Christianity: the divine inspiration of the Bible, the deity of Christ, his virgin birth, his sinless life, his healings and miracles, his vicarious death on the cross, the efficacy of prayer, the literal Return of Christ, and others.

Even as neo-orthodoxy became a substitute for actual orthodoxy in the Mainline Protestant churches, many of their theologians soon wandered away from any meaningful tie to the Scriptures or to the reality of God. By 1966 the cover of Time Magazine would ask "Is God Dead," featuring the Death of God theology of Thomas J. J. Altizer of Emory University, William Hamilton of Colgate Rochester Divinity School, and Paul van Buren of Temple University."[104] As liberal theological educators infected a generation of mainline Protestant pastors with such heresy, they effectively distanced their churches from the rising revival and missed the opportunity to participate meaningfully in the Awakening. Millions of Christians began to leave their churches and flock into the rising Evangelical churches, especially the Pentecostal and Charismatic churches that would persist in preaching the living reality of God with signs and wonders following at the dawn of the fifth Awakening.

**Revivals and Awakenings**

This description of the spiritual state of America from 1945 until around 1965 forces the question of whether the categories of Generational Theory really fit. *While I have taken Generational Theory as the point of departure for this book, I certainly do not advocate for a stubborn insistence that no other ways of thinking about history or about spiritual movements within it are valid. Ultimately, the outpouring of God's manifest presence and grace upon any group of people anywhere at any time does not depend on any definitions imposed upon it by human theorizing.* But the labels "revival" and "awakening" do reliably call to mind distinct phenomena that Christians have experienced in history.

Remarkable revival existed among the churches in the 1950s and Sixties. Major leaders arose and founded powerfully effective missional organizations. Churches sprang up across the country through the church planting efforts of anointed men and women who poured out their lives in sacrificial hard work. Signs, wonders, healings, and miracles followed the preaching of the Word of God. While on the one hand, "the love of many waxed cold" with the advance of skepticism in the Mainline Protestant denominations, the rejection of Charismatic Movement in the historic churches led to their members leaving to attend churches more hospitable to their new spiritual experiences. *The religious experience of America before the fifth Awakening in the Jesus Movement and Charismatic Movement could hardly fit the description of a deserted wasteland!*

*Before an Awakening can result in massive salvations and church growth, revivals and new expressions of Biblical faith must occur to prepare the churches for the reception of the huge waves of new believers that may come with the Awakening.* The Church must enter the next Awakening in robust spiritual health, evangelistic zeal, and remarkable unity. The movement of the Holy Spirit on America's churches in the next twenty years will prepare the church to receive a great harvest along those very lines—just as the rising Charismatic Movement set a track for the "Jesus Revolution" to run on. More than anything else, churches must pray earnestly for revival now. We have not prepared ourselves for a massive move of grace. But we can get ready. An Awakening may tarry, but revival can happen now! So, what will revival look like in our churches in the next twenty to twenty-five years?

# CHAPTER 7

# THE BIBLICAL SIGNS OF REVIVAL

Many Christians today have never personally experienced a great revival and may wonder what revival entails. Revivalist churches over the past 200 years—especially those that follow in the revival tradition of Charles Grandison Finney (1792-1875)—have wondered how to produce a revival and worked to do so when churches have experienced decline and stagnation. Can human effort bring about a true revival? Most Christians realize that while spiritual effort has value, we ultimately cannot force God to send revival by any of our "works of righteousness."

A revival "worked up" by the emotional preaching of enthusiastic evangelists or even "worked at" by the methodical city-wide efforts of revival campaign planners can bring a period of excitement and fruit. Revival efforts can indeed have a great impact on a city or even a region and will often remain in memory for decades. For that matter, many a country crossroads area has experienced religious enthusiasm for a spell that changed the future of families and even clans. No Christian should ever make light of efforts to win souls and revive churches. We should constantly work to revive churches and cities. But churches, not cities, offer the most typical unit of analysis for revival.

*Lasting revival that truly transforms a church and gives it life and vitality and an enduring reality of God's powerful presence usually comes as a surprise.* When Jonathan Edwards wrote an essay to account for the move of God at his church in Northampton, Massachusetts and in the surrounding communities during the First Great Awakening, he titled it as "A Faithful Narrative of the Surprising Work of God." On the other hand, most people recognize that when revival comes, somebody, somewhere has been praying for it.

How can we know that we have entered a true state of revival? What are the characteristics of revival? The early chapters of the Book of Acts offer the best place to look for an example of a true revival. It not only portrays at least twelve signs of revival that graced the life of the Earliest Church, but those signs have typically accompanied the renewal of churches throughout Church history.

Since the revival of Acts 2 marked the founding of the Church, one might not think of it as a "revival." But the history of Israel stands replete with spiritual awakenings and declines. We have this treasure of God—the active presence of the Holy Spirit—in earthen vessels, as Paul said in 2 Corinthians 4:7, and no group of people has ever been able to maintain peak spiritual intensity on a permanent basis—as Generational Theory explains.

The events of Acts 2 represented the ultimate revival of Biblical faith and the beginning of its spread from Jews to Gentiles. It illustrates what happens when people experience a fresh wave of God's grace that results in spiritual enthusiasm among the faithful and its transmission to unbelievers. Churches that experience revival learn to reach the lost and train believers to carry out the mission of God. They play a huge role at times of societal Awakenings, in which Christians find new enthusiasm and power, millions of unbelievers get saved, and national and even global culture stands affected for decades.

**Twelve Signs of Revival**

The primordial revival of Acts 2:36-47 illustrates twelve consistent signs of revival that have characterized spiritual renewal over the course of church history.

*"Therefore, let all Israel be assured of this: God has made this Jesus, whom you crucified, both Lord and Messiah." When the people heard this, they were cut to the heart and said to Peter and the other apostles, "Brothers, what shall we do?" Peter replied, "Repent and be baptized, every one of you, in the name of Jesus Christ for the forgiveness of your sins. And you will receive the gift of the Holy Spirit. The promise is for you and your children and for all who are far off—for all whom the Lord our God will call." With many other words he warned them; and he pleaded with them, "Save yourselves from this corrupt generation." Those who accepted his message were baptized, and about three thousand were added to their number that day. They devoted themselves to the apostles' teaching and to fellowship, to the breaking of bread and to prayer. Everyone was filled with awe at the many wonders and signs performed by the apostles. All the believers were together and had everything in common. They sold property and possessions to give to anyone who had need. Every day they continued to meet together in the temple courts. They broke bread in their homes and ate together with glad and sincere hearts, praising God and enjoying the favor of all the people. And the Lord added to their number daily those who were being saved.* (Acts 2:36-47)

Note the signs of revival in this passage.
**One: Emphasis on Jesus (Acts 2:36).**

In Acts 2, Peter preached to the crowd gathered at Pentecost about Jesus Christ, crucified, dead, buried, and raised to life again as Lord and Messiah. When revival comes, Jesus becomes the top priority for Christians. When churches preach Jesus, people get saved. New believers keep the faith of churches fresh. Churches do not have to wallow in decline or even in need of revival. Many churches maintain vitality for long stretches of time. When churches keep their focus on Jesus, He will keep showing up in their midst by the power of the Holy Spirit.

When a church gets more interested in things other than Jesus, decadence and decline set in. As wonderful as helping the poor and needy can be when it flows out of love for Jesus and a passion for sharing His love in His Name, humanitarian work can kill a church if Jesus gets pushed into second place. Starting a Christian school can offer a phenomenal ministry to a local community, especially in this serious time of crisis for public schools. But when education becomes the center of a church, Jesus tends to get elbowed out of the center.

Pointing out the moral decline of our society has its place, but it can also become a morbid game of "Ain't it awful" in which condemning sinners becomes more interesting than effectively sharing with them the amazing Good News that Jesus loves them and stands ready to receive them in love, like the Father received the messed-up Prodigal Son in Jesus' famous parable. (Luke 15:11-32). I have even seen churches so excited about the gifts of the Holy Spirit that they forgot the Giver and failed to evangelize the lost.

The list of distractions could go on forever. But there is only one Jesus. The school I lead as president, Northwest University, recently changed our motto to "Jesus First, Jesus Always." We made the change because we wanted the very mention of our name and motto to remind us of the primacy and supremacy of Jesus and declare it to anyone interacting with us. We exist to declare and live out the reality of the Living God, revealed in the person of Jesus Christ, made known in the power of the Holy Spirit. When Christian universities forget that priority, they quickly get sidetracked, and churches do not differ. Even a cursory look at church history in America will tell the story of churches and Christian institutions losing their focus, getting distracted, and fading into irrelevance—because they failed to keep Jesus in first place. But when revival comes, Jesus becomes the focus of attention. People will come and worship him for hours on end, basking in his presence, loving him with their whole hearts. And all of the other signs of revival fall into place.

**Two: Repentance (2:37-38)**

When churches truly put Jesus first, Jesus reveals himself. His holy presence enters the church again. When people have an encounter with the Holy God in Jesus, their sinfulness become suddenly obvious. People fall under conviction as they realize their sinfulness, and they repent. On the Day of Pentecost, when Peter preached Jesus to the people, *"they were cut to the heart and said to Peter and the other apostles, "Brothers, what shall we do?"*

People in America today do not want to hear they are sinners in need of salvation. They do not believe in Hell, so they do not fear ending up there. Most people feel free to do as they please, as long as they do not hurt someone else. Americans, after all, have always held up freedom as our ultimate national value. Indeed, God has given human beings freedom, and God will generally not stop them from exercising their moral and spiritual freedom.

God has no interest in taking people's love by force, since love can never come that way. Love has to come freely, as the ultimate and greatest act of freedom. No amount of legalistic reasoning or condemnation from Christians will convince Americans today that they have any obligation to live by moral rules not chosen by themselves, but rather, imposed by others (including God). No amount of Christian teaching about holiness will convince unbelievers that they should repent, since they have such keen ability to detect hypocrisy in the lives of those who proclaim the rules of holiness but have little sense of their own moral failings.

Only an encounter with the holiness of Christ will "cut the hearts" of unbelievers. When they experience Him in the Spirit-anointed proclamation of the Word, they will immediately become aware of their sin. But when a revival strikes, not only do unbelievers repent, but Christians themselves realize how poorly they reflect the holiness of God, and they repent also.

One of the classic prayers of repentance from the historic liturgy of the church declares, "Most merciful God, we confess that we have sinned against you in thought, word, and deed, by what we have done, and by what we have left undone."[105] That prayer dates back to the 8th Century A.D., and untold numbers of Christians have recited it daily for over a thousand years. [106] In the holiness tradition I grew up in, and in my childish appropriation of it, I found myself getting saved often. No amount of effort on my part could keep me from realizing, in the presence of the Holy God, that my previous offerings of the Sinner's Prayer had failed to render me holy. With maturity, I came to realize that Jesus had atoned for all my sins—past, present, and future—and that his gracious sacrifice and the faith he gave me to believe in it had saved me once and for all. An old hymn expresses it well: My sin, O the Bliss of this glorious thought—my sin, not in part but the whole—is nailed to the Cross and I bear it no more, Praise the Lord, Praise the Lord, O my soul!

As Martin Luther taught, we are *simul justus et peccatur* (justified and sinner at the same time).[107] On this side of eternity, we live constantly in the reality of that paradox. But that doesn't mean that fresh encounters with the Holy God do not move us to repentance. The Lord's Prayer recognizes that we never meet all our obligations (debts) to God and stand in need of God's forgiveness constantly. As 1 John 1:8-9 declares, "*If we say that we have no sin, we deceive ourselves, and the truth is not in us. If we confess our sins, he is faithful and just to forgive us our sins, and to cleanse us from all unrighteousness.*" Christians should live in the constant realization that God has forgiven us. Only the knowledge of God's grace can properly motivate and empower us to do the good works God has planned beforehand for us to do (Ephesians 2:10).

When revival comes, people repent. Perhaps the repentance of Christians has some role in the repentance of unbelievers. Whatever the case, true revival always brings a cut heart, a repentant heart. People experience conviction for their sins and repent. But repentance involves more than just words and confessions. It requires a change of behavior. **In revival, Christians change their lifestyles. They not only walk away from patterns of sin, but they turn their attention away from petty entertainments to spend more time in pursuit of God.** Churches experiencing a revival typically hold services several times per week. Outreach ministries draw more volunteers, prayer meetings see strong attendance. Preaching and teaching go longer as people want more of the Word. But I'm getting ahead of myself.

**Three: A burden for the lost (Acts 2:40)**

*With many other words he warned them; and he pleaded with them, "Save yourselves from this corrupt generation."* When Christians have a fresh experience of Jesus, they have a greater desire to share the Gospel with the Lost. In previous generations, we referred to that desire as "having a burden for lost souls." The Bible does not really use that language to refer to the desire to reach unbelievers, but the word "burden" describes the feeling well.

In Acts 20:31, Paul describes his passion in preaching to the Ephesians with tears: "Remember that for three years I never stopped warning each of you night and day with tears." In revival, Christians ramp up their prayers for people who don't know Jesus, and as their desire to see people saved and Jesus glorified heightens, they will "weep for the lost." If you have not experienced such a burden before, you have never fully experienced a true revival.

People who have not met Jesus are lost. One of the most powerful stories in the New Testament relates the story of Zacchaeus in Luke 19. Luke's powerful writing tells of a man in Jericho *called by the name Zacchaeus.*" The New Testament often mentions "a man *named* So-and-so" or "a man *called* So-and-so," but Luke uniquely combines the two phrases: "There was a man called by the name Zacchaeus." Why does he double up on the phrase, calling attention to the name? He emphasizes the name Zacchaeus, which means "righteous man," and then goes on to explain that Zacchaeus had failed to live up to such a name. *"He was a CHIEF tax collector, and he was RICH."* In other words, he was a thief—a shake-down artist.

Everyone in the First Century would have understood that tax collectors got rich by using false information to extort overpayments of taxes —the excess of which they kept for themselves. They had a special word for such shake-down artists: sycophants. The word originally applied to people who would climb a short fig tree— a sycamore tree—to shake the tree and make the figs (sychoi) fall out so the light would shine on them (phaino). Tax collectors came to be known as sycophants.

When Zacchaeus heard the news of Jesus passing through Jericho, he wanted to see who he was. Maybe he thought he would collect some taxes from him, or maybe he felt intrigued by the reports he had heard of this holy man who healed every disease and sickness. But being a small man (in various senses of the word), he couldn't see over the crowds or push through them to see Jesus. So, he climbed up in a sycamore tree.

As Jesus passed by, he looked up in the tree. If he had said, "Sycophant, come down," the crowd would have roared in laughter and approval. It would have been the perfect insult. There stood the sycophant, the shake-down artist, in a fig tree, ready to do his thing. And Jesus could have chopped his little legs out from under him with such a command. But Jesus had no interest in cutting him down to size any further.

Instead, Jesus looked at him and called him by name: "Zacchaeus, come down." Righteous man, come down. I see you. I know who you are. I know what God wants to make you. I see what your parents prayed for when they gave you that name. Come down. Stop being a shake-down artist and get shaken down yourself.

And down, out of the tree, he came. Luke says he "received Jesus" and opened his home to him, where he would soon stand up and declare, "I'm giving half of my goods to the poor, and if I have cheated (literally, "if I have sycophanted") anyone out of anything, I will pay him back four times." Jesus responded by saying, *"Today salvation has come to this house, because this man, too, is a son of Abraham. For the Son of Man came to seek and to save the lost"* Luke 10:9).

What was lost in this case was the true identity of Zacchaeus. In God's wonderful plan for the life of Zacchaeus, he would not remain a wicked thief, but would become a righteous man, a just man who gave to everyone according to his due. He would not remain a faithless person grasping for money, but would become a child of Abraham, the Father of Faith. Zacchaeus would have never realized his true identity—his truest self—if he had not met Jesus.

When people don't know Jesus, they are lost. They have not just lost Heaven or Eternal Life; they have lost their very selves, and they do not know where to find themselves. Back in the Seventies, the Hippie generation used to say they wanted to "find themselves." They knew their lostness. No one had to tell them. To find themselves they needed to find Jesus, and when they found Him, like Zacchaeus, they found their true identity as children of God, "predestined . . . for adoption to sonship through Jesus Christ, in accordance with his pleasure and will" (Ephesians 1:5).

When Christians get a burden for lost people, they begin to pray for them. They weep for their loved ones who do not know Jesus. They start weeping for the soul of the young woman with the scars and piercings at the check-out counter of the grocery store, for the tattooed young man who mows their lawn, for the desperate migrants who have crossed the border illegally and arrived in their town, for the transgender waitress at that restaurant they stopped going to because, well, you know, nobody wants to feel uncomfortable. They start sharing Jesus more. And when they start sharing Jesus out of a heart broken for the lost, more and more people start getting saved.

**Four: An Increase in Conversions (Acts 2:41, 47)**

On the Day of Pentecost, *"Those who accepted [Peter's] message were baptized, and about three thousand were added to their number that day"* (Acts 2:41). As the days went by, *"the Lord added to their number daily those who were being saved"* (Acts 2:47). When a church experiences a true revival, people keep on getting saved because Jesus keeps getting lifted up. People do not just hear a sermon, they see Jesus.

Years ago, when I served as Academic Dean of the Assemblies of God Theological Seminary, we attended James River Church in Ozark, Missouri. The church had experienced red-hot revival for years and had just moved into a huge new building complex that would accommodate weekly services with many thousands in attendance. The church had started in a storefront which they soon outgrew, so they had to build something. They began to build a church for 2,000, but in the time it took to complete it, they had already passed that number in Sunday attendance. So, they sold the new church and built a new, larger building complex a little further down the highway.

We attended the church for five years, and it grew by 1,000 people each year to reach a weekly attendance of 7,000 by the time we moved to Seattle. Since then, the church has continued to grow, and grow, and grow. They have planted several daughter churches, but they just keep growing. More than 20,000 people now attend the church, with hundreds of thousands participating online, and they have bought new property to build a new main campus. I'll say more about the church later, but it offers an example of continuous revival over decades. In revival, churches and Christians can no longer content themselves to let people live without being confronted with the loving holy presence of Christ.

**Five: A Surge in Callings to Ministry and Missions (Acts 4:20)**

During revival, people sense God's calling to Gospel service, whether in vocational ministry or in greater consecration of their daily life and ministry in what others would see as secular settings. Notice how the signs lead from one to another.

1. Jesus is exalted.
2. People repent when they experience his holiness and grace.
3. The repentant get a burden for lost people, having just escaped from a state of guilt themselves.
4. They start sharing the Gospel with others, and more people experience Jesus, who faithfully responds to the preaching of his Word and will make himself known.
5. The more people come to Christ, the more people receive a divine calling to

ministry and missions.

In the Book of Acts, more and more people answered a call to the ministry of prayer and the word. They felt compelled to preach! In Acts 4:20, Peter and John declared, "we cannot stop speaking about the things we have seen and heard." In Acts 4:29 they prayed that God would give them the privilege of speaking the message of Christ with boldness, with healings, signs, and wonders following (4:30). In Acts 6, the church appointed deacons (Greek *diakonoi* or ministers) to take care of widows and feed the hungry so that the apostles could dedicate themselves to "prayer and the ministry of the Word" (Acts 6:4), but before the chapter ends, Stephen, one of the "waiters of tables" got martyred for preaching the Word.

In Chapter 8, Philip, another of the deacons, went to Samaria to preach to the people there (who get saved and baptized in the Holy Spirit) before the Holy Spirit whisked him away to evangelize the Ethiopian eunuch. Throughout the story, more and more people got called to apostolic service, including Ananias and Paul in Chapter 9 and Barnabas and Agabus in Chapter 11 and the elders of Iconium and Lystra in Chapter 14 and John Mark in Chapter 15 and Timothy and Silas in Chapter 16 and Priscilla and Aquila and Apollos in Chapter 18 and more and more and more as the Gospel spread.

Ephesians 4:11-13 tells us that Jesus gives apostles, prophets, evangelists, pastors and teachers to the church (the "five-fold ministry") to equip the believers for the work of the ministry. Where revival sets in, God calls men and women to serve him—as hard-working believers in all the work of the Church, but especially as servants of prayer and the Word. If men and women, young and old, do not receive a call to the ministry as they passionately share their faith in Christ in daily life, revival has not set in yet.

One of the reasons we have seen a terrible decline in people going to Bible colleges and seminaries stems from the fact that we have spent the last thirty to forty years in Unraveling and Crisis. The churches of America have to swim upstream pretty hard to avoid losing their first love, like the Christians of Ephesus in Revelation 2:4. In that passage, Jesus commends the Ephesian church because of their good works, their labor and patient endurance, their intolerance of evil, and their testing of self-appointed apostles to see if their doctrine and lifestyle was true.

Jesus even recognizes that in all of that, they had not grown weary. But despite all the things they were doing—all the good things—Jesus declares that he has something against them. They have fallen because they have left their first love. If they do not recover that first love, they stand in danger of having "their lampstand removed." In other words, they would stop being a church at all. **When the churches lose their love for Jesus and the preaching of the Gospel, they**

**die out.** When men and women do not perceive the call to the ministry of prayer and the word, the light of the churches fades, goes dim and dies. And that's why we can't wait for an Awakening to dawn. We need revival now!

# CHAPTER 8

# MORE SIGNS OF REVIVAL

**Six: A passion for prayer (2:42)**

In the Revival of the Early Church, we see not only a fervor for sharing the Gospel, but also a passion for prayer. Revival always creates in people a new desire to pray, worship, and meditate on God's greatness in grace and love. Sometimes, even in sleep, the prayers continue as God clears away our distractions and speaks to us in dreams. In Acts 2:42, Luke tells us that the believers "devoted themselves . . . to prayer."

Prayer, of course, has many forms. One great revival leader that I know has told me that most of his time in prayer consists of worship, by which he means "singing to the Lord." His church has experienced revival continuously for 30 years, so his approach apparently works! The rise of recorded music in the 20th Century made it possible for Christians to have access to the work of highly skilled musicians at any time, and a "Praise and Worship Movement" promptly rose, especially gaining steam during the Jesus Movement, when young people followed the example of Martin Luther and Charles Wesley and King David other great psalmists of the past in composing Christian lyrics to grace the melodies and styles of the bars and taverns and worldly venues of their time.

The "Jesus People," as the vanguard of the Jesus Movement called themselves, chose the rock ballad as the principal vehicle of worship music, and the music of their time reflected their passion for Jesus just as they had experienced him. Their music often expressed their passion for opportunities to share the Gospel. They imagined the Return of Christ and sang it with enthusiasm. The music drew their peers to church. And so, today's style of Christian music emerged. A large portion of Christian prayer today happens in concert with the car radio, with smart phones and ear buds, and in "worship services" at church—by which people mean, singing.

In yesterday's Evangelical churches, the pulpit typically occupied center stage, declaring the priority of the Word—just as the sacramental altar occupied the center of attention in Roman Catholic and historic Protestant churches. In today's Evangelical churches, the pulpit has become a small, lightweight, see-through acrylic lectern kept offstage until the worship team finishes singing—if not eliminated altogether in favor of preaching from hand-held notes on an iPad or other tablet or even a smart phone. The paper Bible, as it was once said of Elvis Presley, "has left the building."

**By no means do those changes necessarily indicate anything wrong.** The change that means trouble for today's Church has nothing to do with the absence of a pulpit or of a paper Bible or a pipe organ or a grand piano or any other thing. Times and styles and technologies change. The key missing element from most churches is passionate, spirit-led, intercessory prayer for God's work and God's people.

In Acts 4:24ff, the description of an Early Church prayer meeting should humble us profoundly, down to our core:

*When they heard this, they raised their voices together in prayer to God. "Sovereign Lord," they said, "you made the heavens and the earth and the sea, and everything in them. You spoke by the Holy Spirit through the mouth of your servant, our father David:*

*"'Why do the nations rage*
*and the peoples plot in vain?*
*The kings of the earth rise up*

117

*and the rulers band together*
*against the Lord*
*and against his anointed one.'*

*Indeed, Herod and Pontius Pilate met together with the Gentiles and the people of Israel in this city to conspire against your holy servant Jesus, whom you anointed. They did what your power and will had decided beforehand should happen. Now, Lord, consider their threats and enable your servants to speak your word with great boldness. Stretch out your hand to heal and perform signs and wonders through the name of your holy servant Jesus. **After they prayed, the place where they were meeting was shaken.** And they were all filled with the Holy Spirit and spoke the word of God boldly.*

Whether the church is Baptist or Lutheran or Methodist or an independent Bible church or a Pentecostal church or any other kind, revival brings a Spirit-filled atmosphere of prayer. Notice in Acts 4 how the believers told God what they were experiencing, quoted Scripture in their prayer, called out for the manifestation of signs and wonders, healings, and miracles, and left the meeting profoundly shaken (literally) and empowered by their prayers. In revival, prayer takes on a new dimension.

I mentioned James River Church, my home church in Ozark, Missouri. As often as opportunity permits, I go back there for the Wednesday night prayer meeting. For at least twenty years, that meeting has anchored the church's ministry as the most important meeting of the week. Thousands come each Wednesday for the prayer service in the sanctuary, and 40,000 typically follow the meeting online. In recent years, the church has seen a long wave of healings occur, especially on Wednesday night. I love to pray in that sanctuary, and I go there knowing that I'm going to speak to God and God will speak to me. I love the sound of that church in prayer!

A Century and a half after the revival of Acts 2, Tertullian described the prayer of Christians in his time:

> "We meet together as an assembly and congregation, that, offering up prayer to God as with united force, we may wrestle with Him in our supplications. This *strong exertion* God delights in. We pray, too, for the emperors, for their ministers and for all in authority, for the welfare of the world, for the prevalence of peace, for the delay of the final consummation."

Notice the reported vigor of the prayers offered up by revived Christians in the late Second Century.

Tertullian's description of "strong exertion" in prayer reminds me of the prayers I heard in church as a child. Wednesday night prayer meetings found us up around the front of the church, kneeling in prayer. As we would pray, the pastor and other dear mature saints would circulate among us to pray for us, out loud. Everyone prayed out loud at the same time, because "the Early Church prayed that way." I still remember the feeling of having my pastor's hand laid on my shoulder as he interceded aloud for me—he so certain that God would use me in the future if I would yield myself to God, and I so desirous to obey the Lord.

The energy of those prayer meetings was amazing! The sound of dozens of people all praying aloud may not have seemed "decent and orderly" to the more formal churches in our town, but it carried great power to order our lives. When I occasionally hear such prayer today—the sweet cacophony of everyone praying in one accord, each according to the needs perceived—it still shakes my soul. Pentecostals used to call it "concert prayer" because they thought it sounded like an orchestra tuning up in ordered chaos before a concert.

And when the first revived church prayed, it shook the room where they met. Reminiscent of Isaiah's vision of God in the Temple, where the doorposts of the Temple trembled in the presence of God, reports of revival through the centuries and millennia of the church tell of people trembling before the Lord. One group of revived Christians earned the name "Shakers." Another became the "Quakers." Some bore the ridicule of the epithet "Holy Rollers." When revived

Christians pray, they weep and tremble and cry out in desperation for God's Glory. Prayer these days seems altogether too decent and orderly. But when revival comes, God shakes things up.

## Seven: A Hunger for the Word (2:42)

When revival comes, people want more of the Word of God—more personal Scripture reading and study and more exposure to preaching and teaching from godly leaders. In Acts 2:42, the believers "*dedicated themselves to the Apostles' teaching.*" When the Jerusalem religious authorities commanded Peter and John "*not to speak or teach at all int the name of Jesus*" (Acts 4:18), they boldly replied, "*We cannot help speaking about what we have seen and heard*" (Acts 4:20). The content of the apostolic teaching centered on the Old Testament, explaining how it mysteriously foretold the coming of Jesus and how he fulfilled the Law.

Teachers like Barnabas and Apollos soon came from Cyprus and the Greek intellectual capital of Alexandria (Egypt), home of the famous Library and Wonder of the Ancient World. Paul also came out of the Hellenistic world with a comprehensive knowledge of the Greek translation of the Hebrew Scriptures, but also with rabbinic training in Jerusalem under Gamaliel, giving him a keen ability to make the ancient Hebrew teachings relevant to the Greek-speaking Gentile world.

The passion of the believers—not only in

Jerusalem but everywhere the Gospel reached—sometimes kept them up late into the night. In Troas, Paul "kept on talking until midnight," lit by "many lamps in the upstairs room" (Acts 20:7-8). To get some relief from the hot, full room, a young man named Eutychus sought out a perch in a window. As Paul "talked on and on" (20:9) Eutychus sank into a deep sleep, fell out of the window from the third story and "was picked up dead." Paul, undaunted, "threw himself on the young man and put his arms around him." He raised Eutychus from the dead, went back upstairs, and took a break to eat a meal. Then, "after talking until daylight, he left." We know the believers had a deep hunger for hearing the Word taught, because clearly, they stayed as long as Paul would keep on teaching.

The Calvary Chapel churches that arose from Chuck Smith's ministry during the Jesus Revolution made their fame from the expository teaching of the Bible. Revived Christians want to hear the Scriptures taught. They know that the Holy Scriptures *are able to make [them] wise for salvation through faith in Christ Jesus,"* and that *"all Scripture is God-breathed and is useful for teaching, rebuking, correcting, and training in righteousness, so that the servant of God may be thoroughly equipped for every good work"* (2 Timothy 3:15-17). Revived Christians want more of God, long for holy lives, and yearn for wisdom for making the most of their marriages, raising their children, loving their neighbors, and reaching the lost. They will sit for hours when Spirit-gifted teachers open up the Word of God to them.

The next Awakening will enjoy tools we have never had before. Today's podcasts make the best Bible teaching broadly available, and generally free to anyone with a smart phone. In the coming revivals, Christians will have buds in their ears all the time! But they will still come out to hear anointed Biblical teaching, because they will dedicate themselves to prayer, the manifest presence of God among his people, and the fellowship of believers, just as the Christians in the Book of Acts dedicated themselves.

## Eight:  The Manifest Presence of God (2:43)

All Christians understand God's omnipresence, and they know they can pray anywhere. But in times and places of revival, God's presence becomes obvious, palpable, undeniable among us—whether in conviction of sin, healings, miracles, and signs and wonders, or the manifestation of the gifts of the Holy Spirit (1 Corinthians 12). The revival that occurred at Asbury University in February of 2023 evidenced a public sharing among the people who came there of the same feeling of God's manifest presence. And the histories of revival tell the same story throughout Church history. It sounds self-contradictory, but the omnipresent God sometimes "shows up." Indeed, EVERY experience of revival begins when God shows up in a place and keeps on doing it over time. That encounter creates the revival. It can last for hours, days, weeks, months, years, or decades.

In Acts 2:43, "everyone was filled with awe at the many wonders and signs performed by the apostles." Indeed, "The Acts of the Apostles" tells the story of what the apostles and Christians of the Early Church did in response to the work of the Holy Spirit in their midst. Some have pointed out that we should call the book "The Acts of the Holy Spirit," and for sure, it chronicles those acts.

*Christians who claim that such manifestations of the Holy Spirit ceased with the end of the Apostolic Age interpret the Bible the same way as those who believe in the ongoing miraculous acts of the Holy Spirit: They exegete their experience.*[108] Because they have never fully experienced a true, biblical revival, they assume that no one else has done so. They assume that because God has not answered their prayers for miracles, God no longer answers any such prayers for anyone. But Christians who have experienced the powerful move of the Holy Spirit, making the presence of God manifest in the midst of the believers, know for a fact that miracles have not ceased and that God will do again what God has done before. Various theologians, especially Roman Catholics, have noted que that Martin Luther's doctrine of *sola scriptura* and the early Protestant rejection of contemporary miracles led to the rise of atheism during the Enlightenment.[109] People need a miraculous encounter with God, whether it come through a healing, a miracle, a sign, or simply through the equally miraculous still, small voice of God. Some type of "conversion" may happen on an intellectual level, but regeneration —the new birth—requires a miraculous encounter with God. When the next Awakening arrives —and in the many revivals that will precede it, the manifestation of God's presence among us will come with signs and wonders, healings, and miracles following those who believe (Mark 16:17).

## Nine: Greater Generosity Toward the Work of God (2:45)

Church offerings and other manifestations of personal giving to the work of God greatly increase during revival. Acts 2:44-45 reports: *"All the believers were together and had everything in common. They sold property and possessions to give to anyone who had need."* Wherever the revival spread under the ministry of the apostles, the same generosity broke out. As Paul collected offerings from the Gentile churches to help the famine-stricken believers in Jerusalem, he wrote: *"There is no need for me to write to you about this service to the Lord's people. For I know your eagerness to help, and I have been boasting about it to the Macedonians, telling them that since last year you in Achaia were ready to give, and your enthusiasm has stirred most of them to action"* (2 Corinthians 9:1-2).

In 1975—in the heart of the last Awakening

—my mother and brother took a missionary trip to Colombia and when their group returned home, my family joined them for a church service in Montgomery, Alabama to hear their testimonies. They came home excited about all the Colombians who had come to Christ on their trip, and they were determined to raise enough money to build a church for them. After the people of the congregation in Montgomery heard the stories and the appeal for gifts, they stood one at a time and made their pledges. My father, moved to tears for the lost souls of Bogotá, stood up and said, "I have a coin collection worth $700 at home. I will sell it and give it to help build that church."

Dad and I had gone to the bank many times over several years to get rolls of coins to sort through, culling out the valuable coins for our collection, and $700 felt like a lot of money in 1975. After the service, I asked him, "Dad, how can you sell our coins?" (I thought they were mine too, since I had helped collect them.) I will never forget his answer: "Joey, the souls of those people in Colombia mean a lot more to me than those coins do." And I instantly knew I agreed.

People who have experienced revival live in a happy generosity toward the work of God. They give sacrificially to the needs of the poor, but especially to the mission of sharing the Gospel. When revival comes, the needs of the mission go up, up, up! Churches must get planted. The Gospel must spread. Workers must raise support. And when people give, the love of God spreads among us even more, since "God loves a cheerful giver" (2 Corinthians 9:7).

## Ten: Greater Frequency of Corporate gatherings for Worship, Prayer, and the Word (2:46)

In the revival of Acts 2, the believers "continued to meet together in the temple courts." In the Seventies, we went to church several nights a week and twice on Sunday. Other activities just did not seem to carry as much importance! Petty entertainments had little appeal. Why would anyone stay home and watch a silly television show when they could enjoy the thrilling presence of God among God's wonderful people?

Today's churches see very few people attending mid-week services. Not only have churches cancelled Sunday night services for lack of interest, but now, fewer Americans go to church even on Sunday morning, as documented earlier. I remember well how we explained away Sunday-night services as a relic of our agrarian past, appropriate for life on the farm, but not for city people. We did not need Sunday night church.

And indeed, we do not need it. We do not have to go to church twice on Sunday to remain saved. We don't have to take our kids to Sunday School and attend the adult classes before church. We do not have to show up for prayer meetings on Wednesday nights so our kids can take part in the youth group. We don't have to attend the special meetings for women and breakfasts for men and special programs for boys and for girls. We can go to Heaven at the end of our lives just the same (although possibly without our kids).

But when revival comes, we start wanting Heaven now! We have a passion for prayer, a hunger for the word, and a desire to worship God together with other Christians because the special dimension that corporate worship offers does more for us than listening to canned music on our earbuds. God's manifest presence appears! While we can experience God alone, we prefer being the Church, together. I have often said, "We go to Heaven together with the church, but everyone who goes to Hell goes alone." In revival, Christians want to do life together.

### Eleven:  Increased Fellowship among Christians (2:46)

Not only do the number of church services increase during revival, but Christians begin to meet in homes and at restaurants and other venues to spend time together to share the working of God in their lives. Acts 2:46 records the habit of the Early church of seeking fellowship. *"Every day . . . they broke bread together with glad and sincere hearts, praising God."* They celebrated a "love feast" on their Sunday meetings, but they ate together at other times as well.

Table fellowship brings the joy of food together with the love of the Lord in the blessing of community in a way that few if any other things do. Couples on dates eat meals together for a reason, and happy families eat together for a reason: Sharing food means sharing love. Christians in the midst of revival experience greater love for one another that draws them together frequently and attracts unbelievers to their community. But when churches and Christians go stagnant, *Evangelical faith can easily get reduced to a shallow individualism*. People reckon they do not need the Church to be saved, and they figure that excuses them from church. No one in revival has ever believed that.

## Twelve: Favor with the community (2:47)

While the early Christians saw favor with "all the people," that did not include the Sanhedrin and the Jewish leaders, who immediately began to persecute them (Acts 4:1). Both favor and opposition arise when revival begins. Revival brings great joy to a community, as people find rescue from sinful lifestyles, deliverance from evil spirits, healing from disease, and restoration in relationships.

Families find new joy as parents and children and spouses reconcile with each other. Salvation ripples through the community as people take notice of the changed lives of their family and friends and accompany them to church. But at the same time, mockers will always show up when revival occurs, and opposition from seemingly "religious" people and people in power also increases. In contrast, people in revival exhibit new levels of sincerity and authentic faith. They walk in grace and love. The joy of God's favor overcomes any form of persecution or opposition they may face, and people take notice.

**Not every Christian longs for revival, and some will find it more interesting to criticize the next Awakening and its preparatory revivals than to participate in them.** If anyone would rather criticize a church in revival for whatever imperfections of doctrine or practice they may perceive in them, they have entered a dangerous spiritual place. May God help them!

**More than anything**

Our society has many needs and faces many crises today. People disagree about the best ways to improve our common lot, and indeed, we need a lot of things. But more than anything, we need another Great Awakening in America. It will begin and must begin with the household of faith. As mentioned above, we commonly hear that revival comes as a "sovereign work of God's grace," and the reality remains that we cannot "work up" a revival. We certainly cannot have a Great Awakening across American society that results in massive salvations of the lost by merely urging each other to have one. But **we can pray**.

Prayer has always preceded revival. The Acts 2 revival began with many days of concerted prayer in the Upper Room. Revival has probably never begun in any other way. Some people have been praying for revival for a long time alone. Those who have not prayed for revival should join those who do, now. An Awakening may remain years away, but the time has already come to invite a few fellow believers to join us to pray for revival. **More than anything else, we need to seek God** —for ourselves, our families, our neighbors, our country, and our world.

# CHAPTER
# 9

# THE
# CHURCH OF
# THE FUTURE

As president of a Christian university, I enjoy the amazing privilege of close contact and relationships with today's young Christians, and people often ask me about the future of the church. The old cliché says that "children are our future," but young people in fact determine not only the long future of the church, but also the present and near future. Jesus and his disciples led the birth of Christianity in their youth, and perhaps never in Christian history has a major revival been generated by older people. In fact, revivals emerge when younger people, usually in their twenties, experience a wave of repentance and "first love" for Jesus that drives them to call the whole church to greater fidelity and witness.

**Today's Christian young people generally share much of the typical generational outlook of other Gen Z youth, but nothing in their nature or character will keep them from leading the churches in revival when God begins to pour out grace to prepare the Church for the Sixth Great Awakening over the next couple of decades.** Today's Christian youth love the Lord, and they will answer the call when God gives them the grace to hear it.

So, what will the Church of the Future look like? We already know that. John revealed it to us in Revelation 7:9-10:

> *After this I looked, and there before me was a great multitude that no one could count, from every nation, tribe, people, and language, standing before the throne and before the Lamb. They were wearing white robes and were holding palm branches in their hands. [10] And they cried out in a loud voice: "Salvation belongs to our God, who sits on the throne, and to the Lamb."*

God has already determined the nature of the Future Church and has revealed it to us. **The church of the future will inexorably emerge by the power of God's eternal purpose—a glorious church, without spot or wrinkle (Ephesians 5:27), including all the people groups from all the history of humanity, resplendent in praise with the word of salvation still in their mouths.**

## The Marks of the Church

Since 325 A.D. and the Ecumenical Council of Nicea, Christians have confessed their faith in "One, holy, catholic, and apostolic Church." We see precisely such a church as that in Heaven through the prophecy of Revelation 7:9-11. The Church around God's throne displays exactly the characteristics recognized in the Nicene Creed:

(1) **one** multitude—so indivisible that no one can count it;

(2) **holy**, dressed in the white robes of purity— a glorious church without spot or wrinkle as Paul said;

(3) **catholic**, or **worldwide** because it includes every nation, people, tongue and tribe;

(4) **apostolic**, because it continues to declare the message of salvation in Christ, even in eternity.

Theologians refer to these Nicene and Biblical characteristics as "the marks of the Church." Later this chapter will explain further what it means to confess one, holy, catholic, and apostolic church, but for now it suffices to say that the Church of

Revelation 7 represents in fact the True Church, and to the degree that our churches here and now resemble that final state of the church, they can claim to evidence the True Church.

If we want our local expression of the Church to thrive, we must strive toward the ideal Church of Revelation 7. Not every local church reflects that perfect ideal. Some churches fail on the test of unity; others fall short in holiness; others can hardly claim catholicity, and others fail in apostolicity. No local church has ever reached perfection. Reinhold Niebuhr's thesis in *Moral Man and Immoral Society*—that society tends to magnify the effect of personal evil—suggests that no social group—not even churches—can reach the level of devotion that individuals can live out.

Synods and denominations and other corporate jurisdictions of churches likewise struggle to reach perfection, perhaps in decreasing orders of attainment. But God has given us a model to pattern ourselves on, and we dare not stop striving to realize the ideal. **In the end, God will accomplish what we could not in the Church of the Future that will keep emerging over the decades ahead. The Church, triumphant, will press on to the victory of God, *"and the gates of Hades will not prevail against it"* (Matthew 16:18)**

As Paul wrote in Ephesians 6:12, we struggle *"not against flesh and blood, but against the rulers, against the authorities, against the powers of this dark world and against the spiritual forces of evil in the heavenly realms."* In our time, the onslaught of evil continues to cause *"even the elect to be deceived"* (Matthew 24:24). But we must never forget another passage in which Paul considers the impact of evil on the very structures of our existence:

> *I am convinced that neither death nor life, neither angels nor demons, neither the present nor the future, nor any powers, neither height nor depth, nor anything else in all creation, will be able to separate us from the love of God that is in Christ Jesus our Lord (Romans 8:38-39).*

We will stand against the forces of evil because God will make us stand (Romans 14:4).

## Why the Devil Cannot Prevail

The final victory of the Church—and our own victory if we remain faithful to Christ stands assured. Christ has won the final victory on the Cross. Our enemy always overplays his hand. Because Satan has given himself over completely to evil, rejecting God, the only source of good, his evil has no regulator. He cannot contain his evil nor stop himself from acting wickedly. He believes that if a little evil works, more evil works better. And so, he always goes too far. If he could only have stopped himself from crucifying Jesus—if he had only scourged him, nailed him to the Cross, and then let him go, he theoretically might have frustrated God's plan of Salvation. But he could not stop himself, as God foreknew that he would not do.

Satan does not understand the mystery of God's wisdom and the perfection of his plan. Paul explains, in 1 Corinthians 2:7-9:

> We declare God's wisdom, a mystery that has been hidden and that God destined for our glory before time began. **None of the rulers of this age understood it, for if they had, they would not have crucified the Lord of glory.** However, as it is written:
> "What no eye has seen,
> what no ear has heard,
> and what no human mind has conceived"—
> the things God has prepared
> for those who love him.

And in Romans, Paul declares: "*We know that in all things God works for the good of those who love him, who have been called according to his purpose*" (8:28) and "*in all these things we are more than conquerors through him who loved us*" (8:37).

God will defeat Satan and will bring the Church to victory and will "*present her to himself as a radiant church, without stain or wrinkle or any other blemish, but holy and blameless*" (Ephesians 5:27) in God's own time. No Christian likes to see evil running rampant in our world, but we have the consolation, as Paul wrote in Romans 13:11-12, "*our salvation is nearer now than when we first believed. The night is nearly over; the day is almost here. So let us put aside the deeds of darkness and put on the armor of light."*

**One, Holy, Catholic, and Apostolic Church**

Every expression of the Body of Christ imperfectly but distinctly displays the marks of the Church, and the future Church will not fail to do so. **First of all, the Church of the Future will remain one Church,** made up of members from many denominations and congregations.

Over the past one hundred years, especially since the Edinburgh Missionary Conference of 1910, many theologians have written about the scandal of today's divided church.[110] The Ecumenical Movement sought to address the division of Christianity that emerged as a result of (1) Great Schism of 1040 that finally divided the church into Catholic and Orthodox branches and (2) the Protestant Reformation that crystalized in the publication of Martin Luther's 95 Theses in 1517. The Ecumenical Movement failed, as liberal Protestantism generally denied the essential claims of the apostolic kerygma (1 Corinthians 15:3)—especially the literal, bodily Resurrection of Christ—and its eventual embrace of Marxist revolution and its rejection of Biblical authority made it impossible for faithful churches to share communion with the radical church leaders who sought to lead the Church into apostasy.

Rather than coming together in a Global fellowship of doctrinally orthodox denominations, world Christianity, especially in America, has become atomized into a vast collection of independent, non-denominational churches as the historic denominations decline. In the Pacific Northwest, where I live and work, people see the assertion of denominational identity as *gauche.* Churches may belong to a denomination, but they don't usually advertise it in their name. If anyone wants to know where a person goes to church or what denomination they grew up in, he or she must ask very specifically.

Northwest University proudly maintains a denominational identity as part of the Assemblies of God, but our sponsoring denomination has charged us not only with serving their members, but also with offering their best gift to the rest of the Body of Christ. So, we avoid any claim that our denomination has a superior truth or that we are better than other denominations. In my own case, as a fourth-generation member of the Assemblies of God, I am loyal to it not only because I agree with its doctrinal and missional distinctives, but because of the long family and friendship ties I enjoy within it. Having a denominational home can offer wonderful benefits. At the same time, our faculty and student body include Christians from a wide variety of denominations and churches, and we come here to serve God together in unity.

With apologies to those theologians who consider the denominational divisions of Christianity a scandal, I would assert that denominations have played a very healthy role in Church history and in the present. Denominations have marshalled large groups of people across nations to work together for the Kingdom of God. They have provided specific doctrinal positions and explanations for them that have allowed people to confess their faith in a full-throated way, with conviction, rather than just standing around not knowing what to believe. They have exercised valuable moral and doctrinal discipline that has helped ministers avoid their worst temptations or stopped them when they fell into destructive patterns of sin or error. They have blessed, and will continue to bless the Church, to the degree that they avoid sectarian division and a claim to supremacy vis-à-vis other Christian organizations. The same holds for independent churches.

C. S. Lewis, the great proponent of Mere Christianity—the basic beliefs and practices that Christians have held in common since the earliest forms of the Church—very clearly identified himself as "an ordinary layman of the Church of England."[111] He did not see Mere Christianity as a substitute for membership in a particular church. He wrote:

> I hope no reader will suppose that "mere" Christianity is here put forward as an alternative to the creeds of the existing communions—as if a man could adopt it in preference to Congregationalism or Greek Orthodoxy or anything else. It is more like

a hall out of which doors open into several rooms. If I can bring anyone into that hall, I shall have done what I attempted. But it is in the rooms, not in the hall, that there are fires and chairs and meals. The hall is a place to wait in, a place from which to try the various doors, not a place to live in.

Whether we choose membership in a local church that belongs to a denomination or opt for an independent church, we should hold our particular beliefs humbly in service to and fellowship with those Christians who may differ on matters not essential to salvation.

We should believe in the importance of deep conviction and cheer every church and denomination on to greater consecration and service, even as we seek the most perfect unity possible in our congregational expression. In the end, the Church on earth can only approximate the heavenly state of the Church. Although we have not built the New Jerusalem in America yet, as William Blake imagined doing in England, we can see glimpses of Heaven from our churches.

**A Holy Church**

The Church of the Future will remain a holy church, but just as the Church has always struggled to live out its oneness, holiness will continue to challenge us. The word holiness, in fact, has a different definition when applied to God than it does in application to people and things. To simplify the great theologian Rudolph

Otto and his magisterial book, *The Idea of the Holy,* God's holiness emanates from the unlimited divine numinous power.[112] God has appeared in holiness to people of every nation and culture in the world, and the concept bears a remarkable similarity everywhere. Otto views holiness as an "*a priori* element" of religion, "with its own independent roots in the depths of the human spirit itself."[113]

When human beings encounter the Holy, they experience a double mystery: what Otto called the *mysterium tremendum* and the *mysterium fascinans.* The former afflicts humans with an overwhelming, *awful* fear of God as they experience a power that they do not feel worthy to experience and thus perceive as an existential threat. The latter *awe-filled* mystery fascinates and transfixes us, so that even if we desire to flee from the threat of God, we cannot bring ourselves to leave the compelling divine presence.

Kenneth Graham, captured the experience of God's holiness beautifully in a passage from The Wind and the Willows in which Mole and Rat encounter their god:

Rat!" he found breath to whisper, shaking. "Are you afraid?"
"Afraid?" murmured the Rat, his eyes shining with unutterable love. "Afraid! Of *Him*? O, never, never! And yet—and yet —O, Mole, I am afraid!"
Then the two animals, crouching to

the earth, bowed their heads and did worship.[114]

In our age, Christians hardly ever mention the "fear" of God, but anyone who has ever had an experience of God's holiness understands how the fear of God and the love of God require each other and inspire us to live holy lives before God.

Some people seem to have an aura of holiness around them. They inspire the greatest respect and reverence while simultaneously attracting people like a magnet attracts iron. One of those people for me was the late Rev. Desmond Evans, pastor of Bethesda Community Church in Fort Worth, Texas. A Welshman who immigrated to the United States as a young man, he lived a life of remarkable service to God and humanity, and his spotless life will always challenge and inspire me. Many people feared him as much as they loved him, but they never wanted to miss an opportunity to spend time with him.

In this sense, holiness refers not so much to sinlessness as to a certain moral force that emanates from a person. That force can seem forbidding or inviting according to the source and the context. C.S. Lewis tells the story of a truly holy fictional woman in Heaven in his book, *The Great Divorce*, a certain Sarah Smith of Golders Green. He describes her as a woman who, while enchanting men, inspired them love their wives more. As a sort of spiritual mother, she motivated children to love their parents more. In loving animals, she gave them life "through the abundance of life she had in Christ."[115] In such a story, we come to understand that holiness consists not merely in a state of being, but in a dynamic force that emanates from that state, full of joy and power and love. Make no mistake about it: time spent in the presence of God increases our holiness, and sin erodes and even destroys that holiness. Our holiness always exists in relation to God's holiness and our fellowship with it.

Usually, when people ascribe holiness to an object, they refer to the fact that the thing has been "set apart" for holy use. Objects used in worship services, such as communion chalices or plates, crosses adorning an altar, and indeed, the Cross upon which Jesus died. We might call people holy when they have set themselves apart for God's service. But the sad fallibility of people thus set apart reminds us that holiness goes beyond mere function.

People and churches have always struggled to define and live out the holiness of the Church. Years ago, many Pentecostal and Holiness churches seemed to define holiness in legalistic or functional terms, compiling a list of behaviors considered either sinful or conducive to sin. People sometimes sought holiness by obeying those rules—a much easier task than actually seeking God, abiding in God's presence, and walking in the holy power of the God's Spirit.

Reaction in the 1970s and Eighties against

the legalism that had gained so much ground among Conservative Christians in the early decades of the Twentieth Century has led to a situation where we seldom teach about holiness or exhort people to holiness anymore, and many churches and individuals seem to have abandoned all rules, leaving people with a sense of moral freedom that provides no protection from sin. Libertinism can never serve as an antidote to legalism. The True Church hates sin and will not ignore it. Holiness transcends moral codes, but it always includes moral living. But churches and people struggle to realize the ideal of holiness that marks the True Church.

Churches should encourage their members to love God and seek God's face, opening their lives to the power of the Holy Spirit and the positive force of holiness, and they should take two approaches to dealing with sin. First, we have a clear statement of moral principles based on Biblical truth that we declare as our standard. Having such a standard does not and cannot ensure the sinlessness of our community, but it does present a challenge to us all to live up to Biblical standards. We should expect Christians to live up to the behavioral standards of our communities.

In contrast Paul outlines a posture of tolerating behaviors in unbelievers that we would not accept in the Church:

*I wrote to you in my letter not to associate*

*with sexually immoral people—not at all meaning the people of this world who are immoral, or the greedy and swindlers, or idolaters. In that case you would have to leave this world. But now I am writing to you that you must not associate with anyone who claims to be a brother or sister but is sexually immoral or greedy, an idolater or slanderer, a drunkard or swindler. Do not even eat with such people. What business is it of mine to judge those outside the church? Are you not to judge those insides? God will judge those outside* (1 Corinthians 5:9-13).

God will bless efforts to maintain integrity within the Church as well as efforts to share our faith in Christ with those who have not yet come to know him.

The inherent danger all Christians face when they admit unbelievers to their circle means that the influence goes both ways. Christians can influence unbelievers, but unbelievers can influence Christians as well. Our desire for holiness must keep us always vigilant to ensure that we remain close to Jesus, full of the Holy Spirit, and separated from activities that grieve the Holy Spirit and drain us of the attractive power of holiness. But remember also the double mystery at the heart of holiness that includes the inspiration of reverence. We must adopt no form of holiness that sacrifices one of the mysteries to the other—for example, a condemning, judgmental style that radiates no power of love.

**A Catholic Church**

As most Christians know, the use of the theological term *catholic* does not refer only to the "Roman Catholic Church." The word "catholic" (*katholikos* in the original Greek) means, literally, "according to the whole," derived from the Greek word's *kata* (according to) and *holon* (whole). The phrase primarily means that the Church should include Christians from the whole world.

When God established the Migration Mandate, "fill the earth," in Genesis 1:28, the command ensured the realization of the full flowering of human diversity that will eventually come together in the great multitude of the redeemed in Heaven (Revelation 7:9). Migrating to fill the earth entailed the full development of variety encoded in the human genome by God. As people left Eden (and Babel!) to fill the earth, skin tones, cultures, nationalities and every category of difference among humans would emerge. But since the Age of Discovery that began in the late 15th Century, and especially in our postcolonial times of globalization, that emergence has come back together in the global melting pot, in which people from all nations have migrated to all nations.

Never before have so many people representing so much ethnic diversity lived together in the same countries and cities around the world. What once may have seemed like a reality that could only exist in Heaven has become the SOP (standard operating procedure) of the urban and increasingly, the suburban church. In churches throughout the United States today, Christians of every denomination and variety enjoy the catholic diversity of the Church directly on a daily basis.

**An Apostolic Church**

Finally, the Church of the Future remains an apostolic church, wholeheartedly committed to the Gospel and to reaching the world for Christ. The Roman Catholic tradition defined the apostolicity of the church as deriving from "apostolic succession." That idea traced the laying on of hands in ordination through an unbroken chain from the First Century until today. Such a line of succession does exist in Roman Catholic, Orthodox, and most Protestant churches, but the apostolicity of the Church does not derive merely from it.

Some Evangelical Protestant churches would define apostolicity as "following in the apostolic teaching" (Acts 2:38)—and no doubt, faithfulness to the teaching of the Bible, and especially of the New Testament, makes up an important part of apostolicity. But true apostolicity requires a rock-solid commitment to obeying the Great Commission. The word "apostle" comes from the Greek verb *apostolos*, which means "envoy" or "sent one." *The apostolicity of the Church comes from the Commission for which Jesus sent it into mission.* (Indeed, "mission" comes from the Latin verb *mitto*, which means "I send" just like the Greek verb *apostello*.)

Churches that declare the salvation wrought on the Cross by Jesus Christ to all the world exhibit true apostolicity, and every local church must strive to live as an apostolic church. That means we send and receive missionaries, live out our values of evangelization, and train workers in our churches to take the Gospel to every corner of the world, but especially to the closest corners of our neighborhoods and towns and cities and to the country crossroads where people meet.

**The Church of the Sixth Great Awakening**

Every local church in America and around the world should commit itself to fulfilling the ideal of one, holy, catholic, and apostolic church. In my work as an educator observing today's students, I have learned the following things about what the future church will look like and how we should address its needs.

**The Church will remain One**

The Church of the Sixth Great Awakening will have a greater post-denominational character than we have ever seen. By no means does this mean that denominations will face irrelevance. Our relationship with the Assemblies of God denomination at Northwest University offers a terrific example of the usefulness of having a "home team" to work with. But the lines between the churches will never return to the level of hardness they have known.

Denominations played an important sociological function in the settlement of the American frontier, as denominational identity played an important role in creating the social boundaries that held pioneer clans together. At the same time, doctrinal confessions became hardened, serving as a defense against losing young people to other clans. Because such clans played an essential role in keeping communities together, people placed a much greater emphasis on doctrinal agreement than the faith itself required. Christianity functions perfectly well without every Christian agreeing completely on every point of doctrine. As Paul said, *"we know in part"* (1 Corinthians 13:9). In today's America, pioneer clans no longer play any meaningful role in our society, and Christians need continually new connections to succeed, rather than unnecessary, hardened boundaries. For more discussion of this phenomenon, see my book, *The Kingdom Net: Learning to Network Like Jesus*.[116]

In the coming Awakening, new and old denominations will still exist, and independent churches will continue to proliferate, but Christians will display greater unity than we have ever seen since the earliest days of the Church. And just as the Book of Acts demonstrates, division will always play a role in the Church as well, as the Enemy sows discord and even as our fallen humanness creates power struggles among us.

## The Church of the Sixth Great Awakening will also be Holy

Like the church in all times, the church of the future will struggle to define and live out Christian holiness. Young people today in particular face vulnerability in as much as recent postmodern generations abhor the exclusion of anyone. Like the past several generations before them, they find it harder and harder to judge anyone else.[117] The public schools have often had a bigger role in shaping their moral beliefs than the church has had.

Nevertheless, many young people love the Lord and study the Scriptures to learn how to please God rather than taking all their moral cues from their schoolteachers and classmates. They want to belong to churches that have God's favor, and while they may experiment with more permissive churches, their hunger for the real presence of God will lead them back to preference for churches that hold up a clear standard of moral behavior drawn from God's Word in the Holy Scriptures. Imagine a new generation of Christians who manage to love people despite their differences, while at the same time powerfully living up to the standards of Biblical holiness.

In the Greek mythology of Homer's *Odyssey*, Scylla and Charybdis appear as two monsters that lived on opposite sides of a sea passage.[118] Sailing too close to one side put ships in danger of Scylla, while wandering too far to the other side brought Charybdis into play. Ships needed to sail a course right through the middle of the passage to guarantee their safety. The story symbolized the danger of extremes. As for holiness, the extremes are legalism on one side and libertinism on the other.

Legalism used to lead to much hypocrisy in the demand for all to achieve Christian perfection, alienating many while ruining faith for others. Now the danger lies more on the side of libertinism—having no standards at all and accepting sinful behavior under the excuse that no one has a right to judge. An old saw among Christians properly protests, "I'm not a judge; I'm a fruit inspector." We have no right to point fingers at others and pretend that we have reached perfection, but we have every duty to recognize that not every way of life produces godly and pleasing and healthy results. So, we must adopt godly standards for ourselves and our families and churches.

In the run-up to the next Awakening, some churches will continue to capitulate to the values of the world. But we've seen throughout church history—and especially in recent years as Mainline Protestantism has shrunk drastically—

what happens to such churches. They lose God's favor, and they fade away as people leave them to seek out God's presence and the victory over sin that comes with God's help and the support of the Body of Christ. In contrast, the revived churches of the Sixth Great Awakening and its preceding years will not fail to teach Biblical holiness to their people. They will continue to promote biblical morality and standards in their community lifestyle expectations. Like their predecessors, they will fall short of God's ideal, but they will never quit striving for God's presence and God's holiness. When we abide in God, we will not fail to reflect God's holiness in our lives.

## The Church of the Sixth Great Awakening will be catholic

America will continue to become more diverse. The lowest birthrates in history that we have generated today mean that immigration rates will remain high for many years to come. Follow the money: Population => business => money. In the years ahead, the electorate will demand an immigration policy that regulates immigration legally and provides for a growing economy, vastly reducing the shadow system that currently exists outside the law. In the future of America, churches that fail to attract a diverse membership will fail the test of legitimacy among today's and tomorrow's young Christians.

The hard racial divisions that once characterized America have begun to melt away, provoking louder and louder voices (and harsher complaints about racism) among those who seek power and wealth from stoking division. But intermarriage among the races has increased among all social classes in America, and racial rivalries will lessen considerably over the next twenty years. Since 1967 when interracial marriage became legal in all fifty states, the percentage of interracial marriages has increased from 3% to 19%--about one in five American marriages.[119]

In 2021, Gallup Organization found that 94% of American adults approve of marriages between Black people and White people. Only 4% approved in 1958.[120] The increasing approval of interracial marriages, even among the most historically divided races, together with the respect for diversity among young people today, suggests that America's future divisions will center more around social class and income level than on racial identity. Nevertheless, Churches will continue to become more and more "catholic" in America's future.

But catholic means more than just "international" or "interracial." It also means that we preach the "the Gospel according to the whole"—that is, the Full Gospel. Pentecostal churches have preached for a century that the full Gospel declares Jesus as our Savior, Healer, Spirit-Baptizer, and Soon-Coming King. Today's young people know that a full Gospel must also result in full bellies. They care deeply about social justice and meeting the needs of people holistically. They will demand a gospel "without a hole in it."[121] The Churches of the Sixth Great Awakening will place a greater emphasis on evangelism that today's churches do, but they will not abandon concern for suffering people at home and around the world. In all previous Awakenings in America, the churches have risen to the challenge of addressing the needs of the poor, and the coming Awakening will not differ from those of the past in this crucial aspect of Kingdom work.

## The Church of the Sixth Great Awakening Will Be Apostolic

**It** became abundantly clear during the pandemic that the ministry of the churches uses technology more than ever. In the past Awakenings in America, Christians have always marshalled the latest technology to spread the advance of the Gospel. (Think of Billy Graham and Oral Roberts using television and radio.) The young people of today love technology, and the next generation will enjoy even greater technological power.

Recently, the COVID-19 pandemic forced even the most tech-shy churches to learn how to broadcast their services on Facebook and YouTube and Zoom, and they would have never met the challenge had it not been for the teenagers and twenty-somethings in their churches who taught them how to do it. As the age of Artificial Intelligence dawns, now is not the time to abandon technology. Churches have already begun to use artificial intelligence for translating their services to different languages almost simultaneously.

Growing churches now and in the future will maximize artificial intelligence technologies for every-day contact with the people who visit and attend our churches. Church apps need maximizing, systems need expanding. Gen Z stands ready to serve the propagation of the church like never before through technology, and as they take the reins of ministry leadership in the coming age of revival, they will do even more.

Gen Z also has a strong missionary impulse and calling. No generation has ever cared more about the oppressed people at home and around the world than the Millennial Generation did. A hardy, heroic lot, they show more willingness to put their lives on the line in mission than the last few previous generations did. They will lead Gen Z to rise and meet the apostolic challenge, and the churches need to prepare to send them forth. As they mature, they will see the advent of the Sixth Great Awakening, and they will faithfully bring their experience to the rising generation to continue the apostolic advance of the Church.

# CHAPTER 10

# PREPARING FOR THE NEXT AWAKENING

In this book I have drawn a clear distinction between revivals and Awakenings. Once again, a revival happens when God sovereignly, by God's own good pleasure, pours out the Holy Spirit on people, usually on churches, and energizes their faith and their desire so that they evidence the enthusiasm of the Early Church in living out Christian faith together and reaching unbelievers and reclaiming backsliders. An Awakening happens when a society turns its attention to spiritual things after a long period of prosperity and victory and the emptiness that inevitably follows it. An Awakening may or may not result in revived churches and large numbers of new Christians. The Sixth Awakening that America will experience in the 2040s may or may not bring the Church to its finest hour. **What we do about it will matter.**

If American churches do not experience revival in the years leading up to the next Awakening, they will miss out on the greatest opportunity in history. Even now, churches around the world continue to experience revival. The Church continues to burgeon in Africa and China and Latin America and Asia. Revival can come to our churches in America also, but we must seek God to receive it. To those who will immediately offer a *solo fide* objection, I can only respond that my Christian tradition believes firmly in the value of moral and spiritual effort, even if that effort cannot produce salvation, righteousness, or revival without God's sovereign response, according to God's sovereign Will.

**Pray for Revival**

Lonely prayer warriors probably accomplish more for the Kingdom of God than we could ever realize, and private sessions of prayer certainly set the framework for our personal spiritual lives. But Christian prayer must always include a corporate dimension. We pray much better in groups than any of us can pray alone. The model of prayer that Jesus taught his disciples assumes that people will pray together. "OUR Father . . . give US this day OUR daily bread, and forgive US OUR trespasses, as WE forgive those who trespass against US, and lead US not into temptation, but deliver US from evil." If all your prayer happens in solitude, you can improve on it by joining others.

Jesus expressed his love for prayer groups in Matthew 18:18-20. Notice the plurality of the pronouns, made explicitly plural in English to match the originals in Greek:

*Truly I tell y'all whatever y'all bind on earth will be bound in heaven, and whatever y'all loose on earth will be loosed in heaven. Again, truly I tell y'all that if two of y'all on earth agree about anything they ask for, it will be done for them by my Father in heaven. For where two or three gather in my name, there am I with them"* (My translation).

Jesus clearly indicates his will for us to pray together in groups. People who seriously want to see renewal in their lives and revival in their church will put together groups to pray with. Why not name such groups "Next Great Awakening Prayer Groups"? Make worshipping and praising Jesus the first order of business. Pray for God to reveal his Will and exercise his Reign in your church and the other churches of your neighborhood, town, country, state, and country. Pray for God to pour out the Holy Spirit on leaders and on the whole church. Pray for people to evidence the signs of revival:

- God's manifest presence with signs and wonders and healings and miracles;
- repentance;
- passion for prayer;
- hunger for the Word;
- a burden for the lost (with specific names listed);
- increased numbers of new converts;
- desire for fellowship;
- increased numbers of people called into the ministry of prayer and the Word;
- greater generosity to God's work;
- more frequent gatherings of the Body; and
- favor with the community around us.

All other preparations for revival have a secondary role. Prayer comes first, and without it, we will squander the next Awakening and miss out on the greatest opportunity in the history of the Church.

**Live in Repentance**

Even as I finish writing this chapter, the Governor of Tennessee has signed a bill passed overwhelmingly in the state legislature declaring 30 days of fasting and prayer for the month of July 2024. The legislature asked churches to read the bill publicly on June 30, asking people to:

- Examine our lives in light of God's Word and confess of our sins,
- Acknowledge that we, as the Church, have failed to stand for the principles of God, ask for His Forgiveness and Mercy,

and commit to stand firmly on those principles going forward,

- For those who are able, join in prayer and intermittent fasting as a means of demonstrating our desire for repentance. [122]

The bill forthrightly recognizes the spiritual crisis in Tennessee, stating the need for repentance, prayer, mercy, and healing as follows:

A RESOLUTION to seek God's hand of mercy healing on Tennessee.

WHEREAS, our State and Nation suffer from violence committed upon our citizens by our citizens; and

WHEREAS, our State and Nation suffer from violence committed upon our citizens by non-citizens; and

WHEREAS, acts of violent crime in our schools are unacceptable; and

WHEREAS, human trafficking is an unacceptable and violent evil in our State, enslaving lives and violating the core values of our Creator-endowed rights to life, liberty, and the pursuit of happiness; and

WHEREAS, drug addiction overwhelms our families, our government finances, our workforce productivity, as well as our healthcare and our law enforcement resources; and

WHEREAS, deadly fentanyl flows uncontrollably across our southern U.S. border resulting in the deaths of Tennesseans; and

WHEREAS, Driving Under the Influence, drunk driving, results in great pain and injury for Tennessee families; and

WHEREAS, we have approximately 9,000 children in need of foster care, indicating a brokenness in many Tennessee homes; and

WHEREAS, evidence of corruption in our federal government stands to impact every Tennessean; and

WHEREAS, our National and State Founders trusted in the omnipotent hand of Providence to guide and bless our land; and

WHEREAS, over decades, these leaders called our people to seek out the Creator's favor by issuing proclamations like the one from John Adams on April 15, 1799:

[This day] be observed throughout the United States of America as a day of solemn humiliation, fasting, and prayer; that the citizens on that day abstain, as far as may be, from their secular occupation, and devote the time to the sacred duties of religion, in public and in private; that they call to mind our numerous offenses against the most high God, confess them before Him with the sincerest penitence, implore his pardoning mercy, through the Great Mediator and Redeemer, for our past transgressions, and that through the grace of His Holy Spirit, we may be disposed and enabled to yield a more suitable obedience to his righteous requisitions in time to come; that He would interpose to arrest the progress of that impiety and licentiousness in principle and practice so offensive to Himself and so ruinous to mankind; that He would make us deeply sensible that "righteousness exalteth a nation, but sin is a reproach to any people." [Proverbs 14:34]; and

WHEREAS, we hold that our Founders correctly acknowledged Truth in their words; and

WHEREAS, we hold that "Except the Lord keep the city, the watchman waketh but in vain" (Psalm 127:1); now, therefore,

BE IT RESOLVED BY THE HOUSE OF REPRESENTATIVES OF THE ONE HUNDRED THIRTEENTH GENERAL ASSEMBLY OF THE STATE OF TENNESSEE, THE SENATE CONCURRING, that the period of July 1, 2024, through July 31, 2024, be recognized as a time of prayer and fasting in Tennessee.

BE IT FURTHER RESOLVED, that we recognize that God, as Creator and King of all Glory, has both the authority to judge and to bless nations or states.

BE IT FURTHER RESOLVED, that we, as public servants in the Tennessee General Assembly, seek God's Mercy upon our land and beseech Him to not withdraw His Hand of blessing from us.

BE IT FURTHER RESOLVED, that we recognize our sins and shortcomings before Him and humbly ask His Forgiveness.

BE IT FURTHER RESOLVED, that we ask the Lord Jesus to heal our land and remove the violence, human-trafficking, addiction, and corruption.

BE IT FURTHER RESOLVED, that we ask that the Holy Spirit fill our halls of government, our classrooms, our places of business, our churches, and our homes with peace, love, and joy.

BE IT FURTHER RESOLVED, that we call upon all those who are physically able and spiritually inclined to do so to join in a thirty-day season of prayer and intermittent fasting as we begin a new fiscal year as a means of seeking God's blessing and humbling ourselves to receive His Grace and Mercy, transforming ourselves, our communities, our State, and our Nation.[123]

While such a bill hardly lacks precedent in

American history, its humility and faith offer a shocking message in our time. Far from violating the "establishment clause" of the First Amendment to America's constitution, it favors no particular religious organization and compels no religious activity. Church and state remain appropriately separate, but with the state urging the churches to do what they can appropriately do to help in what government has failed to do.

Such governmental encouragement to the churches will increase over the years to come, and just as Eisenhower's championing of faith against the threat of communism resulted in an increase in church attendance—along with the outpouring of the Holy Spirit on the churches and on Christian evangelism and the ministry of healing —we have good reason to expect revival in the church over the coming years—if we step in to help the government and the people by leading in repentance.

Remember again the words of the reference to 2 Chronicles 7:14 in the Tennessee bill:  *if my people, **who are called by my name**, will humble themselves and pray and seek my face and turn from their wicked ways, then I will hear from heaven, and I will forgive their sin and will heal their land.*  Remember the practice of godly Daniel, who "*turned to the Lord God and pleaded with him in prayer and petition, in fasting, and in sackcloth and ashes,*" "*speaking and praying, confessing [his] sin and the sin of [his] people Israel and making [his] request* to the Lord [his] God for his holy hill" (Daniel 9:3, 20). When God's people take the lead, confessing their own sins first and recognizing second the sins of their people, God will smile upon us and hear us, mighty to save.

No revival will come without prayer and repentance, and no greater sin could accrue to us than to refuse the call of our governmental authorities for us to pray for them. As Samuel said when the people of Israel rejected his leadership and called for the anointing of a king, "*As for me, far be it from me that I should sin against the Lord by failing to pray for you.*"

The time to pray has fully come!

## Take the Bible Seriously

An appalling ignorance of the Bible plagues today's Church. For the Millennials and Gen Z to pastor the Sixth Great Awakening effectively, they will have to ramp up their knowledge of the Holy Scriptures. Today's children will have grown into young adults by the time the Awakening dawns, and along with the previous two generations, they will suffer from truly woeful ignorance if we do not get them excited about God's Word in the next twenty years. As they preach and teach, they will directly compete with artificial intelligence readings of the Bible. Often, the AI will have greater knowledge of the text than they do, even as sometimes it will fail terribly to understand, but nevertheless with seeming authority.

Today's and tomorrow's preachers will have to "up their game," but the good news should encourage us. We have the best resources ever available to create a love for the Word. The advance of archaeological knowledge and the understanding of the Biblical World that we have gained in the past 50 years put us in a position to understand and teach the Bible better than ever before. No excuse will absolve us of the failure to learn deeply about the Bible, just as we will find no substitute for seeking God to communicate its message and its real power in the anointing of the Holy Spirit.

Taking the Bible seriously means approaching it with our intellect as well as looking to it for "life hacks." That means we will look to the Bible for insight into God's nature (theology) as well as for ethical and moral guidance. Doing those things well requires a careful reading of the Bible in its ancient context as well as thoughtful consideration of its application to our current realities. Most people never get past a childish reading of the Bible. While that kind of approach has its value, and Jesus does say in Matthew 18:3 that adults should have child-like faith, we err greatly if we do not realize the difference between a childish understanding of the Scriptures and the value-added "second naivete" that faithful adults bring to the Bible.[124]

Between childhood and adulthood, everyone passes through adolescence. During that time of life, as the pioneering psychologist Eric Erickson has taught us, we pass through a stage known as "individuation," in which young people must come to their own sense of identity. Teenagers today face the same temptations young people have always faced—handling peer pressure, finding faithful friends, managing their sexual urges, and deciding what work they will pursue in life—but they face intellectual challenges related to faith in the context of the Information Age, in which almost all the learning produced in the history of the world stands available to them in their pocketed smart phones. If the preacher says something they doubt, they can fact-check him or her during the sermon. The recent movement known as "the new atheism" has carried out a radical campaign to flood the internet with arguments against Christianity. Young people can find counter arguments to almost anything we can proclaim as truth in seconds.

Preachers and teachers today cannot get away with plagiarism, sloppy thinking, made-up facts, and bloviation as they could in the past. When teenagers check their facts and conclude that they lack foundation for what they so confidently proclaim, the credibility of the Gospel begins to erode for them. Preaching or teaching the Bible poorly, without a strong understanding of it, can unwittingly convince young people that the Bible is morally wrong, outdated, unscientific, or even cruel.

Christians need to study the Bible now more than ever before to present it well to the next generation of children and adolescents, as well as to the millions of Gen X, Millennial, and Gen Z Christians who have rejected the Bible due to poor handling of it on the part of Christian elders. At the same time, we have never had more access to outstanding resources for learning. Today's young Christians and the rising next generation will prefer to get their Bible teaching online, because they tend to trust digital media more than more "analog" forms of instruction. Just as the Internet provides a flood of anti-Christian information, it also features the best Bible teachers in the World. But we can only imagine now the impact that Artificial Intelligence will have on how the next generation engages through software.

More and more podcasts become available each year that feature outstanding Bible teachers sharing the most recent scholarship at no cost. I like to listen to the Bema Podcast by Marty Solomon and the Bible Project Podcast led by Tim Mackie. I also love the "Ask N.T. Wright Anything" podcast, which features powerful discipleship lessons from the most prominent New Testament scholar in the World—a deeply Evangelical, Spirit-filled Anglican bishop. As mentioned above, The Bible Project also offers phenomenal video instruction on YouTube and on their website. Many people who prepare for ministry these days have chosen to skip formal study, to the great detriment of Bible teaching in the Church. But choosing not to attend a Bible College or Seminary no longer necessarily means forgoing a solid understanding of the Bible.

No Christian should ever take their family to Washington DC without visiting the Museum of the Bible at least once. In a city filled with the finest museums in the world, the Museum of the Bible has put together amazing, sophisticated, easy-to-understand exhibits to teach people of all ages about the Scriptures. Whatever fascinating exhibits the Smithsonian Institution or the National Gallery or the Holocaust Museum may offer—and every American should visit them at least once if not often—a visit to the Museum of the Bible can make a greater and more lasting spiritual impact on children and teenagers.

I have had the privilege of studying at some of the finest academic institutions in the world across a wide variety of fields, from history to psychology to sociology to politics to foreign languages to economics to management and other subjects, but nothing has impacted my life more than the academic study of the Bible. Everyone studying for pastoral ministry deserves the opportunity to study the Bible, theology, and Church history in a formal academic setting. As expensive as college and seminary can seem, amateurism in the pulpit will exact a steeper price. Every Christian in America needs to take Bible study seriously now in preparation for coming revivals and the Sixth Great Awakening that will give us a chance to change the world for Christ.

**Share the Gospel with Everyone**

One of the things I learned as a pastor is that people need an opportunity to accept Christ. I found many years ago that no matter what my sermon topic addressed, an invitation to receive Christ made for a perfect conclusion to the service. On many occasions, people visit a church specifically for an opportunity to accept the Lord. If they do not get that opportunity, they can leave disappointed, distracted, or derailed. A battle for their soul rages in their hearts and minds, and they need to make a decision for Christ and receive instruction about what to do.

Years ago, as a college student, I had the opportunity to hear the great evangelist C.M. Ward preach at a local church in Springfield, Missouri. Ward became nationally famous for his preaching on the Revivaltime broadcast on the ABC Radio Network from 1953 to 1978, but I had never heard him before.[125] He preached a fairly dull sermon that night, and I felt a bit disappointed. When he gave an altar call, no one came forward. Undaunted, he continued to call people forward for what seemed like half an hour. He would not relent. I said to myself, "Let it go, Brother Ward. No one will respond tonight." But he kept going. Finally, something broke loose and dozens of people rushed forward to the altar to receive Christ as their Savior.

I thought about what I had seen that night for a long time, and I concluded that I had completely misunderstood what happens when a minister makes an altar call. People struggle in their minds. Should I go forward? What will happen? Will they embarrass me? Do I have time? Will the people I came here with wait for me? Should I make them wait? Do I really want to change my life? The questions go on without limit. People need the preacher to persuade them to make a decision for Christ. The same principle applies to the context of personal evangelism. People need someone to persuade them.

In no way does pleading with sinners violate their will. They do not have full control of their will! They suffer as captives to sin, under the power of the Enemy. They need someone to help them break free. While a preacher should never trick or deceive anyone into accepting Christ—that territory belongs to the devil—every evangelist should prepare for a spiritual battle as they attempt to lead people to Christ.

Christians today, including me, do not share the Gospel as enthusiastically as we did in the 1970s. In those days, we lived for the opportunity to share our faith in Jesus with anyone who would listen and talk to them about their souls. We could say to ourselves now, "Well, if there were revival at my church, more people would get saved." But what if the reverse is the truth: no revival will emerge until people start getting saved?

Aside from the manifest presence of God, nothing gets a church more excited than new believers, with their testimony of transformed lives and their "first-love" experience of Jesus. If we want to see revival, we should start sharing our faith more broadly, with anyone who will listen. We should invite people to meet Jesus personally. We should plead with those whom we see under conviction for their sins, with people we see the Holy Spirit working on to bring them to Jesus. In the worst case, we will gain experience that will come in handy during the coming revivals and the Sixth Great Awakening. In the best case, we will see people getting saved now!

## Focus on radiant holiness, not rules

When true revival comes to a church, holiness breaks out among its people. People who have encountered the holiness of God repent of their sins and begin to live a new life. Unfortunately, they have too often tried to reduce holiness to a set of rules that they try to impose on everyone else. It never works. As Paul wrote to the Colossians,

> *"Do not handle! Do not taste! Do not touch!"? These rules, which have to do with things that are all destined to perish with*

*use, are based on merely human commands and teachings. Such regulations indeed have an appearance of wisdom, with their self-imposed worship, their false humility and their harsh treatment of the body, but they lack any value in restraining sensual indulgence"* (Colossians 2:21-23).

No one ever achieved holiness by keeping rules, but untold numbers of people have been pushed away from faith in Christ by people trying to impose their holiness code on them.

Instead of merely wearing holiness as a superficial appearance, seek to know Jesus so deeply that the Holy Spirit radiates out of your innermost being. Jesus said, *"'Let anyone who is thirsty come to me and drink. Whoever believes in me, as Scripture has said, rivers of living water will flow from within them.' By this he meant the Spirit, whom those who believed in him were later to receive"*(John 7:37-39). Holiness and its awesome power flow out of us when we have drunk deeply of the Holy Spirit through fellowship with Jesus. The fruit of the Spirit of Holiness—love, joy, peace, forbearance, kindness, goodness, faithfulness, gentleness and self-control —flow out of us in power, and our ego gets lost in our fascination with the person of Jesus and His presence through the Holy Spirit. People so influenced by the Spirit will live out  scriptural morality, but they will do so differently than those who merely follow a moral code.

In the Book of Acts, after Peter and John healed the lame man at the temple gate called "Beautiful," the high priests Annas and Caiaphas who engineered the Crucifixion of Jesus *"saw the courage of Peter and John and realized that they were unschooled, ordinary men; they were astonished, and they took note that these men had been with Jesus"* (Acts 4:13). The conclusion of the high priests did not merely flow out of the time the apostles had spent with Jesus before the Crucifixion. Had they not continued to seek Jesus out and walk in the fullness of the Holy Spirit, they would not have showed up at the Gate called Beautiful to heal the lame man. They would not have spoken with such courage and power. The passage makes it clear that the high priests were **afraid** to do anything to them. Their astonishment and fear of two ordinary men flowed directly from the radiant holiness of their lives and actions.

**In order to prepare for the revivals ahead and the Sixth Great Awakening, Christians today should seek out the presence of Jesus at every opportunity, being continuously filled with the Spirit of Holiness in order to walk in radiant love, joy, peace, and power.**

**Focus on Young People**

Older people have never led in the front lines of revival in the whole history of the church. Undeniably, however, older people have a role to play in a revived church. Like Simeon and Anna at the Temple at the time of Christ's dedication (Luke 2:25-38), they know how to pray! They have wisdom, experience, knowledge, and a long track record of errors to guide them in advising and empowering young leaders. But young people have energy! Despite the holiness and maturity of the prophetess Anna who frequented the Temple, God chose Mary to bear the Christ child over Anna for a reason! Young people have newness of faith and love for Christ. They understand their generation, and they must become the vanguard for reaching it.

The popularity of youth evangelist Billy Graham and his impact through Youth for Christ had a huge impact on American Evangelicalism after World War II. Evangelical Christians in America began to put a huge emphasis on youth ministry during the twenty years that preceded the Jesus Movement, and the young leaders they formed between 1945 and 1968 became the pastors who received the younger new converts who began to flood into their churches in the 1970s and Eighties. The same thing will happen when the Sixth Great Awakening arrives in the 2040s. The Gen Z teenagers and young adults of today who become pastors and church leaders during the next twenty years of revival will either steward the next Awakening and see a massive growth of Christian faith—and with it the saving of the American Experiment—or they will fail to do so.

**The effort we spend in discipling Gen Z now will pay enormous dividends in the future. Universities, Bible Colleges, and churches that disciple young leaders should wake up now to the incredible opportunity they have to shape the future through today's youth.** But discipleship is a two-way street. In order for us to disciple Gen Z, and for them to disciple the next generation, a habit of mutual learning must emerge. As Earl Creps has powerfully described in *Reverse Mentoring: How Young Leaders Can Transform the Church and Why We Should Let Them,* we have to allow young Christians to teach us what we do not know, even as we teach them what we know.[126]

Discipling young people means more than teaching them to read the Bible and discipling them in prayer, although these elements remain indispensable. Real discipleship means teaching patterns of behavior, which demands time spent together involved in God's work. My father discipled me as a child by taking me with him in his many labors for the Gospel. We did everything from working on church maintenance chores to setting up for activities to passing out Gospel tracts from door-to-door visitation to ministering in the local jail.

My mother made sure I got opportunities to sing solos in church from the age of five or six and paid for music lessons to make sure I could play instruments at church. She taught me to make puppets for the children's ministry and then to write scripts and act out the puppet shows. She involved me in helping her teach other children. Throughout my teen years she served as the nurse every summer for weeks on end at our denomination's statewide Youth Camp, taking me along and making sure I got uncounted hours of exposure to the best and most inspiring youth ministers in the nation.

Other adults in the Church made sure I got experience teaching younger kids in Sunday School and leading other youth in the Youth Ministry, giving me opportunities to sing in choirs and lead the adult services in worship, in groups and by myself. Other members of the church would invite me to mow their lawns and would spend time talking to me. One of the most impactful experiences I had as a young teenager was spending a Saturday with my pastor, the late Bobby Lowery, as we cleaned the church in preparation for Sunday services. He took me out for a hamburger at lunch time and spent time talking to me about my life and future, and he had an impact on my dreams to follow his example in ministry that never faded away.

Today's church has learned the hard way—and in a way that churches in my youth sadly had not learned—that we must have background checks and guard rails to protect children from predators at church. But we will make a great mistake if we cut off all opportunity for older Christians to spend time discipling younger ones. Not every young Christian today—and far less than in my day—has two parents deeply committed to their discipleship, and even in that case, the influence of other Christians remains very important.

Christians should spend time discipling the next generation, but they should also spend money. No young person that God has called to Church ministry and has been approved by their congregation as a candidate for ministry should ever have to forego formal education because of a lack of funding. Investing in the training of the next generation of ministers remains a crucial responsibility of Christians, and members of churches should express significant generosity in helping young people they have grown to love and admire.

The founders of America's first Bible College —now Harvard University—understood that truth when they explained in 1636 that they founded the college, "dreading to leave an illiterate ministry to the churches, when our present ministers shall lie in the dust." For that reason, my family has endowed a permanent scholarship at Northwest University in honor of my father, the late James Jackson Castleberry, to ensure that young ministers in training get financial help until Jesus comes.

**Focus on renewal first, not revival**

In this book, I have offered specific

definitions for the terms renewal, revival, and awakening, focusing on the personal, community, and societal expressions of the refreshing work of God. As we prepare for the Sixth Great Awakening, our concern should focus first on the personal dimension. An old hymn declared, "Let there be peace on earth, and let it begin with me." Revival will always begin after individuals have made a covenant with God and have sought God out personally. When that renewal gets shared in community and God's presence breaks out in community, revival happens. When an Awakening presents opportunity and revival renews the conditions of the Early Church in a community, major shifts in faith can occur on a societal level.

But it always starts with individuals who get in the right place with God. Noah found grace and saved the human race. Abraham believed God, and his family succeeded in blessing every family on earth. Samuel heard from God and led Israel to victory. David sought to build the Lord's Temple, and the Lord built him a house— an eternal dynasty. Esther stepped up when the right time arose, and her people were spared from destruction. Jesus submitted himself to baptism, and from that moment the Spirit of God came upon him in power, and he launched the ministry that would take him to the Cross, where he would save the whole world. What will God do if you follow hard after him with your whole heart?

Start the focus there.

**Focus on Revival, not Awakening**

Finally, as we prepare for the Sixth Great Awakening, we should focus on the community around us, not on society. An Awakening will occur when societal forces produce it. That much remains inexorable, and it will happen when it happens. Will we have prepared ourselves and our churches to make the most of it? Along the way, Paul's advice remains relevant: *"Pray that I may proclaim it clearly, as I should. Be wise in the way you act toward outsiders; make the most of every opportunity. Let your conversation be always full of grace, seasoned with salt, so that you may know how to answer everyone"* (Colossians 4:4-6).

When Paul says, *"Make the most of every opportunity,"* he has a specific kind of opportunity in mind. In truth, we cannot make the most of *every* opportunity. The concept of opportunity cost recognizes that taking advantage of one opportunity necessarily means foregoing other opportunities. Our time and attention have limits. The Greek phrase translated here as "make the most of every opportunity" (*ton kairon exagorazomenoi*) contains two important concepts. The first word, *kairos*, means "opportunity" or "an opportune moment." It inherently recognizes that not all times or moments have the same value. Some moments offer greater possibilities than others.

In dealing with people outside the faith—

specifically in dealing with their spiritual need—some moments present themselves as pregnant with opportunity to bring a person or a group into the Kingdom of God. When we see such moments, we have to act! The other concept, translated as "make the most," comes from the Greek verb *exagorazo*. The Greek word *agora* means "market." The preposition *ex* means "out of." When those two words combine into a verb, it literally means "get out of the market." In other words, "buy." But the word *exagorazo* suggests an aggressive buying, such as in the phrase "corner the market," or "utterly buy up all of it." When we see a moment of opportunity with someone outside the faith, a moment to lead them to Christ or to pray for their healing or to serve them in a way that moves them closer to Jesus, we should spend ourselves totally in the effort.

In one of Jesus' parables, he uses a similar word: *"Again, the kingdom of heaven is like a merchant looking for fine pearls. When he found one of great value, he went away and sold everything he had and bought it"* (Matthew 13:45-46). Known as the Pearl of Great Price, this parable refers to the other side of the evangelistic equation. When someone perceives the value of the Kingdom of God, they should completely sell out and "buy" the Kingdom. The word for "buy" in this passage is *Agorazo*—a softer version of *Ex agorazo*. But the two verbs carry the same meaning in the two passages. Just as we expect unbelievers to "sell all they have" to "buy" the Gospel of the Kingdom, we as Christians should even more aggressively "buy in" every time we see an opportunity to share the Gospel.

Making the most of the Sixth Great Awakening and its penumbra of revival in the next twenty years will cost us everything. While grace comes to us freely and salvation costs us nothing, it costs us everything to fully engage in the work of God's Kingdom. There has never come a greater time than now to sell out completely and devote ourselves to the maximization of the years ahead, reaching one soul at a time until the deluge hits during the golden years of the Millennials, the prime of life of Gen Z, and the young adulthood of the coming generation not yet born.

# A PRAYER FOR REVIVAL

"We have heard it with our ears, O God; our ancestors have told us what you did in their days, in days long ago." (Psalms 44:1 NIV) "Lord, I have heard of your fame; I stand in awe of your deeds, Lord. Repeat them in our day, in our time make them known; in wrath remember mercy." (Habakkuk 3:2).

O Lord, hear our cry!  Revive your church again. We have failed to pray.  We have neglected your Word.  We have given up meeting together often for worship and fellowship.  We have not wept for the lost people around us.  We have tolerated the advance of evil and immorality and the deterioration of our culture and our nation. We have sought out comfort and entertainment and leisure, and we have discarded the godly work ethic of our parents and grandparents.  We have pointed the finger at others while denying our own faults.  We are utterly unworthy of your blessing.

Yet we have heard what you did for others in their times. Human failure is old, but your grace and mercy are older and have always come to save the day. Rise up again, O Lord! Pour out your Holy Spirit on these dry bones! Convert us anew!

*"Have mercy on us, O God, according to your unfailing love; according to your great compassion blot out our transgressions. Wash away all our iniquity and cleanse us from sin. Cleanse us, and we will be clean; wash us, and we will be whiter than snow. Let us hear joy and gladness. Hide your face from our sins and blot out all our iniquity. Create in us a pure heart, O God, and renew a steadfast spirit within us. Do not cast us from your presence or take your Holy Spirit from us. Restore to us the joy of your salvation and grant us a willing spirit, to sustain us. Then we will teach transgressors your ways, so that sinners will turn back to you. Open our lips, Lord, and our mouths will declare your praise. Our sacrifice, O God, is a broken spirit; a broken and contrite heart you, God, will not despise* (Psalm 51:1-17)."

# Appendix: Generational Cycles in the History of Judah

My interpretation of generational cycles in the history of the kings of Judah as related in the Bible suggests the following pattern:

| Generational Cycles in the History of the Kingdom of Israel/Judah | | | | |
|---|---|---|---|---|
| Generation | Years | King(s) | Cycle | Events |
| 1 | 1050-1010 BC | Saul | High | Military Victory and Economic Advancement |
| 2 | 1010-970 | David | Awakening | Ark brought to Jerusalem, David's Psalms written, Temple |

| | | | | |
|---|---|---|---|---|
| | | | | planned |
| 3 | 970-930 | Solomon | Unraveling | Temple completed, spiritual decline, idolatry |
| 4 | 931-913 | Rehoboam | Crisis | War and secession of the Northern Kingdom |
| 5 | 911-870 | Abijah | High | Alliance with Aram, victory over Israel, Cities built |
| 6 | 870-848 | Jehoshaphat | Awakening | Godly king leads army into battle with worshippers in the lead |
| 7 | 848-835 | Jehoram, Ahaziah, Athaliah | Unraveling | Evil kings, Assassinations, Athaliah's usurpation, |
| 8 | 835-796 | Joash | Crisis | Defeat, loss of the sacred objects of the Temple |
| 9 | 796-767 | Amaziah | High | Military victory over Edom by obedience to God |
| 1 | 767-748 | Uzziah | Awakeni | Righteous |

| 0 | | (Azariah) | ng | king seeks God, becomes powerful, but ends reign in religious arrogance and leprosy, beginning the next cycle |
|---|---|---|---|---|
| 1 1 | 748-732 | Jotham | Unraveling | Relative prosperity under godly king, but people "continued their corrupt practices" |
| 1 2 | 732-716 | Ahaz | Crisis | Wicked king, sacrifices son in the fire, military defeat, idolatry |
| 1 3 | 716-687 | Hezekiah | High and Awakening | Successful rebellion against Assyria, Scriptures collected |
| 1 4 | 687-642 | Manasseh | Unraveling | Idolatry and atrocity return, crisis begins |

| 1 5 | 642-640 | Amon | crisis | Short reign leads to an 8-year-old king, Josiah |
|---|---|---|---|---|
| 1 6 | 640-608 | Josiah | High/ Awakeni ng | Book of the Law found, religious reform |

These possible cycles of society in Judah seem to follow the order predicted by Generational Theory. Reigns do not perfectly follow the time periods of generational cycles, as kings may serve for forty years or more, and the Bible does not report everything that happened in Judah during the reigns and generational successions. It would appear that the cycles ran very fast after Josiah and suffered significant disruption and eventual cessation, as regular generational cycles are not automatic when a society enters its end phase.

Such an analysis may seem like cherry-picking facts to fit the Procrustean bed of the theory, but if readers do not see a "repeating" of the cycles, they may at least hear a "rhyming" of them.[127] By the end of the 400 years considered, Judah's history had essentially run its course, falling under the domination of large empires and other civilizational forces that put an end to the regularity of generational cycles.

## *About the Author*

**Joseph Castleberry** is the sixth president of Northwest University, a Christian college in Kirkland, Washington. The author of several books, he preaches frequently at churches  and conferences around the world, especially on the topic of the Holy Spirit. He also speaks and writes in the media about moral, spiritual, and societal issues. Before coming to Northwest University in 2007, he served as Academic Dean of the Assemblies of God Theological Seminary in Springfield, Missouri and as a missionary to Latin America, where he planted churches and served in community development, ministry training, and theological education over a period of twenty years.

A graduate of Evangel University, he also completed the Master of Divinity degree from Princeton Theological Seminary and a Doctor of Education degree in International Educational Development from Columbia University in 1999.

Dr. Castleberry and his wife Kathleen have three daughters: Jessica (with her husband Nathan Austin), Jodie (married to Roberto Valdez), and Sophie (married to Andrew Bender), plus seven grandchildren and counting.

Readers are encouraged to contact Dr.

Castleberry at joseph.castleberry@icloud.com.

# Acknowledgements

As Marcus Tullius Cicero said: *"Multas amicitias silentium diremit."* (Silence has destroyed many friendships.) So, I do not want to fail to give credit to the many friends who helped me get this book to print. I especially want to thank Dr. Raul Sanchez, who motivated me to write in May 2024 by inviting me to speak in Spanish at the Parc 55 Hilton Hotel in San Francisco, California to the Central Pacific Ministry Network Ministers Retreat on the topic of generational ministry. The enthusiastic reception by pastors of the ideas developed here inspired me to write a book, and the first draft came out only a month later, which quickly became the Spanish version of the book as well.

An informed reader can tell from the title of the book alone how much I owe to the late William Strauss and to Neil Howe, without whose brilliant, creative, and bold theory of history the book could not have come forth. I have interpreted their theory and made liberal use of it, working mostly from memory and interpretation as I adjusted it and employed it to fit my own purposes. Where it varies from their own work, they were probably right.

Thanks to Edgardo Montano, my teacher and editor for 35 years who read the Spanish translation and offered valuable corrections. I acknowledge the contribution of Eliezer Oyola, my first and most important Spanish teacher and also thank the many Latino friends who tolerated my first 10,000 hours of practice in the language. Thanks also to Steve Bostrom, Dr. Joshua Ziefle, Kathleen Castleberry, Edgardo Montano, Sarah Drivdahl, Ben Sigman, and other early readers who made helpful comments and edits to improve the readability and argument of the book. Dr. Ziefle, a professional church historian who does far more meticulous, careful, academic work in his own writing, kindly tolerated my analysis of history in the service of predicting the future, and he deserves no blame for it. Jim Edwards, my professor at Evangel University some forty years ago, made an indelible impression on the way I write, as did editors Liz Heaney and Steve Halliday who worked with me on previous books.

As always, thanks to Ted Terry, who has always given me great advice about the best venues for publishing my books. Thanks also to Kindle Direct Publishing, for making it so easy to publish this book and make it available in printed and digital formats.

On the spiritual side, I am grateful to my parents, who raised me in the nurture and admonition of the Lord, and my pastors through the years, who have taught me the faith and inspired me to serve the Lord: Clifton Carney, Bobby Lowery, Tom Bougher, Robert McConnell, Kenneth Rodli, Herschel Hicks, Galen Hertwick,

Jesse and Kay Owens, Paul Tedesco, John Lindell, Darrell Elliott, and Brandon and Di Beals, and Pete Hartwig.

My family, mentioned earlier, makes me happy—and their love and support contributes immeasurably to my motivation to write.

Finally, thanks to the Board of Directors and personnel of Northwest University in Kirkland, Washington for the privilege of serving them as president for the past 17 years and for the liberal toleration and faithful support of my writing habit. What a difference they have all made in my life!

[1] J. Edwin Orr, Prayer and Revival. Available: https://jedwinorr.com/resources/articles/prayandrevival.pdf.

[2] Aaron Earls, Most Teenagers Drop Out of Church When They Become Young Adults, *Lifeway Research,* Jan 15, 2019. Available: https://research.lifeway.com/2019/01/15/most-teenagers-drop-out-of-church-as-young-adults/.

[3] Aaron Earls, Most Teenagers Drop out of Church When they Become Young Adults, Lifeway Research, January 15, 2019. Available: https://research.lifeway.com/2019/01/15/most-teenagers-drop-out-of-church-as-young-adults/.

[4] Daniel A. Cox, Generation Z and the Future of Faith in America, *Survey Center on American Life*, March 24, 2022, https://www.americansurveycenter.org/research/generation-z-future-of-faith/.

[5] Pew Research Center, "Nones" on the Rise, *Pewresearch.org*, October 9, 2012. Available: https://www.pewresearch.org/religion/2012/10/09/nones-on-the-rise/#:~:text=The%20growth%20in%20the%20number%20of%20religiously%20unaffiliated,just%20one-in-ten%20who%20are%2065%20and%20older%20%289%25%29.

[6] Pew Research Center, Religious 'Nones' in America: Who They Are and What They Believe: A closer look at how atheists, agnostics and those who describe their religion as 'nothing in particular' see God, religion, morality, science and more, *Pewresearch.org,* January 24, 2024. Available: https://www.pewresearch.org/religion/2024/01/24/religious-nones-in-america-who-they-are-and-what-they-believe/.

[7] Jason DeRose, Religious 'Nones' are now the largest single group in the U.S. *All Things Considered,* January 24, 2024. Available: https://www.npr.org/2024/01/24/1226371734/religious-nones-are-now-the-largest-single-group-in-the-u-s#:~:text=A%20new%20study%20from%20Pew%20Research%20finds%20that,adults%20than%20%20Catholics%20%2823%25%29%20or%20evangelical

%20Protestants%20%2824%25%29.

[8] Pew Research Group, How the Pandemic Has Affected Attendance at U.S. Religious Services: Stable share of Americans have been participating in some way – either virtually or in person – during the pandemic, but in-person attendance is slightly lower than it was before COVID-19. *Pewresearch.org, March 28, 2023.* Available: https://www.pewresearch.org/religion/2023/03/28/how-the-pandemic-has-affected-attendance-at-u-s-religious-services/.

[9] Jeffrey M. Jones, Church Attendance Has Declined in Most U.S. Religious Groups: Three in 10 U.S. adults attend religious services regularly, led by Mormons at 67%. Gallup.com, March 25, 2024. Available: https://news.gallup.com/poll/642548/church-attendance-declined-religious-groups.aspx.

[10] Billy Hallowell, Dire Projections for Christianity in America Over the Next 50 Yeats Could Have 'Far-Reaching Consequences for Politics, Family Life, and Civil Society', *Faithwire*, September 14, 2022. Available: https://www.faithwire.com/2022/09/14/dire-projections-for-christianity-in-america-over-the-next-50-years-could-have-far-reaching-consequences-for-politics-family-life-and-civil-society/.

[11] Aaron Earls, If the Rise of the Nones is Over, What's Next? Lifeway Research, Jun 3, 2024. Available: htttps://research.lifeway.com/2024/06/03/if-the-rise-of-the-nones-is-over-whats-next/.

[12] Meagan Saliashvili, Jordan Peterson wrestles with God, *Religious News Service*, February 15, 2024. Available:https://religionnews.com/2024/02/15/jordan-peterson-wrestles-with-god/.

[13] David Brooks, The Jordan Peterson Moment, New York Times, Jan 25, 2018. Available: https://www.nytimes.com/2018/01/25/opinion/jordan-peterson-moment.html.

[14] Olivia Cavallaro, Jordan Peterson's Daughter Mikhaila Comes To Faith In God, Christianity Daily, October 26,

2021. Available: https://www.christianitydaily.com/news/jordan-peterson-s-daughter-mikhaila-comes-to-faith-in-god.html. Heather Tomlinson, Mikhaila Peterson: from psychedelics to faith, *Woman Alive*, 2 November 2022. Available: https://www.womanalive.co.uk/mikhaila-peterson-from-psychedelics-to-

faith/14181.article.

[15] Brandon Showalter, Jordan Peterson talks of Jesus, the Gospel, leading Christian fans to speculate about his faith journey, The Christian Post, Wednesday, March 10, 2021. Available:https://www.christianpost.com/news/jordan-peterson-talks-of-jesus-leading-christian-fans-to-pray-for-his-faith-journey.html.

[16] Tom Holland, I Began to Realise That Actually, In Almost Every Way, I am Christian, Unbelievable? October 28, 2020. Available: https://www.patheos.com/blogs/unbelievable/2020/09/tom-holland-i-began-to-realise-that-

actually-in-almost-every-way-i-am-christian/.

[17] Richard Clements, Evangelizing "Lapsed Atheists," Word on Fire, August 23, 2023. Available: https://www.wordonfire.org/articles/evangelizing-lapsed-atheists/.

[18] Hope Bolinger, What Is Christian Atheism? Christianity.com, November 3, 2022. Available: https://www.christianity.com/wiki/christian-terms/what-is-christian-atheism.html.

[19] Andrew "Drew" McCoy, The 5th Horseman of Atheism is Christian Now (and I don't care), *Genetically Modified Skeptic*, Youtube.com, December 2023. Available: https://

www.youtube.com/watch?v=Kmx1pE2rvKU.

[20] Ayaan Hirsi Ali, Richard Dawkins vs. Ayaan Hirsi Ali: The God Debate. *UnHerd Podcast*, June 3, 2024. Available: https://unherd.com/watch-listen/the-god-debate/.

[21] Katy Perry: my religious parents think Russell Brand is having spiritual awakening, *The Standard*, April 11, 2012, Available: https://www.standard.co.uk/showbiz/katy-perry-my-religious-parents-think-russell-brand-is-having-spiritual-awakening-6510809.html.

[22] For more reports of this trend, see Justin Brierley, A Christian revival is under way in Britain, *The Spectator*, March 30, 2024. Available: https://www.spectator.co.uk/article/a-christian-revival-is-under-way-in-britain/.

[23] Historian Jonathan Butler described the term "First Great Awakening" as "an interpretative fiction," arguing that "the label "The First Great Awakening" distorts the extent, nature, and cohesion of the revivals that did exist in the eighteenth-century colonies, encourages unwarranted claims for their effects on colonial society, and exaggerates their influence on the coming and character of the American Revolution. Jonathan Butler, "Enthusiasm Described and Decried: The Great Awakening as Interpretive Fiction," *Journal of American History* 69:2 (September 1982). Available https://www.jstor.org/stable/1893821?refreqid=excelsior%3Ada9832e58877561f55cefcf4e3354f62.

[24] Disagreement about when particular seasons have occurred point out the subjectivity involved in assigning such interpretations to history.

[25] In this book I have accepted the definition of awakening offered by William Strauss and Neil Howe in *Generations: The History of America's Future*: 1584 to 2069, William Morrow & Company, 1991. For another interesting look at awakenings from a Nobel Prize-*winning economist's point of view, see Robert William Fogel, The Fourth Great Awakening & the Future of Egalitarianism*, University of Chicago Press, 2000

[26] Ted Sorensen, *Counselor: A Life At The Edge Of History*, Easton Press, 2008.

[27] Joseph Bottum, *An Anxious Age: The Post-Protestant Ethic and the Spirit of America*, Image, 2014; Sean Collins, Wokeness: old religion in a new bottle: Joseph Bottum on how the decline of Protestant America fueled the rise of identity politics, *Spiked*, August 14, 2020. Available: https://www.spiked-online.com/2020/08/14/wokeness-old-religion-in-new-bottle/; Daniel J. Mahoney, The Idol of Our Age: How the Religion of Humanity Subverts Christianity, Encounter Books, 2018; Joshua Mitchell, *American Awakening: Identity Politics and Other Afflictions of Our Time*,

Encounter Books, 2020; Joshua Mitchell, A Godless Great Awakening, First Things, July 2, 2020. Available: https://www.firstthings.com/web-exclusives/2020/07/a-godless-great-awakening; Mike Sabo, The Great Awokening: Identity Politics versus Christianity, RealClear Religion, April 12, 2021. Available: https://www.realclearreligion.org/articles/2021/04/12/the_great_awokening_identity_politics_versus_christianity 772348.html#!; David Rozado, Where did the Great Awokening Come From? UnHerd, September 8, 2020. Available: https://unherd.com/newsroom/where-did-the-great-awokening-come-from/; Jennifer Graham, America's 'Great Awokening,' explained: Before you use the word 'woke,' learn how its meaning has changed in the past few years, *Deseret News,* March 23, 2021. Available: https://www.deseret.com/indepth/2021/3/23/22332164/americas-great-awokening-explained-woke-social-justice-racial-justice/; Eric Kaufmann, The Great Awokening and the Second American Revolution, *Quillette,* June 22, 2020. Available: https://quillette.com/2020/06/22/toward-a-new-cultural-nationalism/.

[28] Matthew Yglesias, The Great Awokening: A hidden shift is revolutionizing American racial politics—and could transform the future of the Democratic Party. *Vox,* April 1, 2019. Available: https://www.vox.com/2019/3/22/18259865/great-awokening-white-liberals-race-polling-trump-2020.
[29] Jonathan Chait, The Great Awokening is Over, But Trump Might Revive It: Conservatives are still angry at 2020, don't understand Biden wasn't president then. *The Intelligencer, New York Magazine ,* Jun 26, 2024. Available: Available: https://nymag.com/intelligencer/article/donald-trump-joe-biden-great-awokening-george-floyd.html.

[30] Disagreement about when particular seasons have occurred point out the inherent subjectivity involved in assigning such interpretations to history. Historical interpretation is inherently subjective, and it either resonates with other observers or it does not. Social phenomena of all kinds are subject to individual interpretation. My reading of history in this case is tied to my greater emphasis on the experience of American

Christianity,

[31] Neil Howe, *The Fourth Turning Is Here: What the Seasons of History Tell Us About How and When This Crisis Will End*, 2023. Available: https://a.co/eoYw9xy.

[32] Charles Snyder, D.L. Moody and the genesis of the Student Volunteer Movement, *D.L. Moody. Center,* May 29, 2020. Available: https://moodycenter.org/articles/d-l-moody-and-the-genesis-of-the-student-volunteer-movement/. Estimates of how many missionaries produced by the movement vary wildly, from 8,000 to 40,000.

[33] Readers who want to explore American church history in greater detail should explore Mark Noll's excellent volume, *A History of Christianity in the United States and Canada*, Eerdmans, 2019. The scope of this book has not allowed for a deep dive into earlier periods of Awakening and revivals. Those who want to focus on the role of youth in revival history will delight in J. Edwin Orr, *Campus Aflame: Dynamic of Student Religious Revolution*, International Awakening Press, 1971, which chronicles the role of college students in revival throughout history.

[34] Andrew L Yarrow, *Look: How a Highly Influential Magazine Helped Define Mid-Twentieth-Century America*. Potomac Books, 2021.

[35] In physics, the Big Bang Theory posits a definite beginning of time, but physics cannot ultimately determine whether the universe will end or recycle itself with a contraction and new bang.

[36] A. N. Mouravieff, *The Christian Remembrancer*, Vol. 10, "A History of the Church in Russia." London, James Burn Publishers, 1845, 265.

[37] Marx, Karl. (1869). *The Eighteenth Brumaire of Louis Napoleon* (Chapters 1 & 7 translated by Saul K. Padover from the German edition of 1869; Chapters 2 through 6 are based on the third edition, prepared by Friedrich Engels (1885), as translated and published by Progress Publishers, Moscow, 1937. Available: https://www.marxists.org/archive/marx/works/1852/18th-brumaire/.

[38] Neil Howe, *The Fourth Turning is Here: What the Seasons of History Tell Us About How and When This Crisis Will End*, Simon & Schuster, 2023.

[39] William Strauss and Neil Howe, *Generations: The History of America's Future, 1584 to 2069*, Quill, 1991.

[40] Mark Noll, A History of Christianity in the United States and Canada, Eerdmans, 1992, 167.

[41] Pew Research Center, Global Christianity— A Report on the Size and Distribution of the World's Christian Population. December 19, 2011. Available: https://www.pewresearch.org/religion/2011/12/19/global-christianity-exec/.

[42] Neil Howe, The Fourth Turning is Here, Simon and Schuster, 2023.

[43] George Friedman, *The Calm The Storm Before the Calm: America's Discord, the Coming Crisis of the 2020s, and the Triumph Beyond*, Doubleday, 2020.

[44] George Friedman, *The Next 100 Years: A Forecast for the 21st Century*. Doubleday, 2009.

[45] Joseph Adinolfi, Stocks are extremely overvalued according to an indicator favored by Warren Buffett, MarketWatch, July 9 2024. Available: https://www.msn.com/en-us/money/markets/stocks-are-extremely-overvalued-according-to-an-indicator-favored-by-warren-buffett/ar-BB1pHgtW?ocid=BingNewsSerp.

[46] Andrew Thurston, The World Is Going Bust: What Is the Sovereign Debt Crisis and Can We Solve It? *The Brink*, August 7, 2023. Available: ttps://www.bu.edu/articles/2023/what-is-the-sovereign-debt-crisis-and-can-we-solve-it/.

[47] David J. Lynch, Soaring U.S. debt poses risks to global economy, IMF warns, The Washington Post, June 27, 2024. Available: https://www.msn.com/en-us/money/markets/soaring-us-debt-poses-risks-to-global-economy-imf-warns/ar-BB1p1oX6?ocid=BingNewsSerp.

[48] Gabriela Berrospi, Hyperinflation: Is The US Following Venezuela's Path? Forbes, May 21 2024. Available: https://

www.forbes.com/sites/forbesfinancecouncil/2024/05/21/
warning-signs-of-hyperinflation-is-the-us-following-

venezuelas-path/.

[49] Jason Dempsey and Gil Barndollar, The All-Volunteer
Force Is in Crisis: A half century after the induction of the last
draftee, America's military faces tough choices. The Atlantic,
July 3, 2023. Available: https://www.theatlantic.com/ideas/
archive/2023/07/all-volunteer-force-crisis/674603/.

[50] This reckoning depends on, but does not exactly
match that proposed by Neil Howe, *The Fourth Turning Is
Here: Reimagining the Future*, Simon & Shuster, 2023. My
interpretation has a more ecclesio-centric basis than that of
Howe.

[51] Jesus Revolution, directed by John Erwin and Brent
McCorkle, featuring Joel Courtney, Jonathan Roumie, Kelsey
Grammer, Anna Grace Barlow, and Kimberly Williams-
Paisley, Lionsgate, 2023. Also see Greg Laurie and Ellen
Vaughn, *The Jesus Revolution: How God transformed an
Unlikely Generation and How He Can Do It Again Today*, Baker
Books, 2018.

[52] Ethan Sacks, X doesn't mark the spot: As Millennials
and Baby Boomers feud, a generation is left out:
Generation X has largely earned a reputation for being
cynical and disconnected politically. *NBC News*, November
24, 2019: Available: https://www.nbcnews.com/news/us-
news/x-doesn-t-mark-spot-millennials-baby-boomers-feud-
generation-n1082381.

[53] Robert D. Postman, Bowling Alone: The Collapse and
Revival of American Community, Simon & Schuster, 2000.

[54] Jean M. Twenge, *Generations: The Real Differences Between
Gen Z, Millennials, Gen X, Boomers, and Silents—and What
They Mean for America's Future.* Simon and Schuster, 2023;
Mark McCrindle and Emily Wolfinger, *The ABC of XYZ:
Understanding the Global Generations*, McCrindle, 2009; *John
Palfrey and Urs Gasser, Born Digital: Understanding the First
Generation of Digital Natives. Basic Books, 2008;* Chloe Combi,
*Generation Z: Their Voices, Their Lives*, Hutchinson, 2015.

[55] Caitlyn Gibson, 'Baby on Board': How a cutesy decal

embodies the enduring terror of parenthood, Washington Post, May 1, 2019. Available: https://www.washingtonpost.com/lifestyle/on-parenting/baby-on-board-how-a-cutesy-decal-embodies-the-enduring-terror-of-parenthood/2019/04/30/a6559e58-6a80-11e9-be3a-33217240a539_story.html.

[56] Joseph Serwach, The Latchkey Kids: The Least Parented Generation: Born 1965 to 1980, the Latchkey Kids watched themselves 'home alone' while our parents paid the costs of 1970s hyperinflation (like today?), *Medium*, June 13, 2022. Available: https://medium.com/the-partnered-pen/the-latchkey-kids-the-least-parented-generation-b38a6fb2942c. For an example of Gen X resentment of the Baby on Board signs, see Annalisa Merelli, You probably don't know the real story behind Baby on Board signs, *Quartz*, October 6, 2014. Available: https://qz.com/275987/you-probably-dont-know-the-real-story-behind-baby-on-board-signs.

[57] Jeff Cunningham, Why Is Gen Z So Depressed—Overprotective Parents, Thunderbird School of Management. Available: https://thunderbird.asu.edu/thought-leadership/insights/why-generation-z-so-depressed-overprotective-parents. Greg Lukianoff and Jonathan Haidt, The Coddling of the American Mind: How good intentions and bad ideas are setting up a generation for failure, Penguin Press, 2019.

[58] Jonathan Haidt, *The Anxious Generation: How the Great Rewiring of Childhood is Causing and Epidemic of Mental Illness*, Penguin Press, 2024.

[59] New research finds that pandemic learning loss impacted whole communities, regardless of student race or income. *Center for Education Policy Research, Harvard University*, May 11, 2023. Available: https://cepr.harvard.edu/news/new-research-finds-pandemic-learning-loss-impacted-whole-communities-regardless-student.

[60] Ayalet Sheffey, Gen Z is the New Threat to the American College Experience, *Business Insider*, December 23, 2023. Available: https://www.businessinsider.com/gen-z-value-of-college-higher-education-student-debt-tuition-2023-12.

[61] New National Survey Finds Pandemic-Driven Shifts in Gen Z Priorities for Education and Work Persist Fourth Annual "Question The Quo" Study Shows Strong Belief in Education After High School; Vast Majority

of Teens Feel Unprepared to Choose Their Future Path, ECMC Press Release, June 27, 2023. Available: https://www.ecmcgroup.org/news/group/new-national-survey-finds-pandemic-driven-shifts-in-gen-z-priorities-for-education-and-work-persist.

[62] Jack Flynn, 25+ Gen Z Statistics [2023]: Tech Preferences, and More, Zippia, May 9, 2023. Available: https://www.zippia.com/advice/gen-z-statistics/#:~:text=To%20dive%20deeper%20into%20how%20Gen%20Z%20interacts,an%20average%20of%2035%25%20of%20their%20day%20online.

[63] Carmen Miranda, Generation Z: Re-thinking Teaching and Learning Strategies, Faculty Forum, April 24. Available: https://www.facultyfocus.com/articles/teaching-and-learning/generation-z-re-thinking-teaching-and-learning-strategies/.

[64] Aimee Pearcy, Gen Zers are shutting down accusations that they're 'lazy' by listing all the reasons why they don't want to work, *Business Insider*, September 15, 2023. Available: https://www.businessinsider.com/gen-z-responds-to-accusations-that-theyre-lazy-and-dont-want-to-work-2023-9.

[65] Russell Goldman, Here's a List of 58 Gender Options for Facebook Users, *ABC News*, February 13, 2014. Available: https://abcnews.go.com/blogs/headlines/2014/02/heres-a-list-of-58-gender-options-for-facebook-users.

[66] Debra Soh, What's Driving Gen Z's Aversion to Sex?, *Newsweek*, Oct 12, 2021. Available: https://www.newsweek.com/whats-driving-gen-zs-aversion-sex-opinion-1638228#:~:text=It%27s%20important%20to%20remember%20that%2085%20percent%20of,create%20an%20overall%20sense%20of%20malaise%20and%20disillusionment.

[67] Andrew Benson, Alcohol consumption on the decline for Gen Z, studies suggest, *Global News*, January 14, 2023. Available: https://globalnews.ca/news/9411516/alcohol-consumption-decline-gen-z/.

[68] Megan Carnegie, Gen Z: How young people are

changing activism, *BBC*, August 8, 2022. Available: https://www.bbc.com/worklife/article/20220803-gen-z-how-young-people-are-changing-activism.

[69] Christoph Kastenholz, Gen Z And The Rise Of Social Commerce, *Forbes*, Apr 14, 2022. Available: https://www.forbes.com/sites/forbesagencycouncil/2021/05/17/gen-z-and-the-rise-of-social-commerce/.

[70] Jim Davis and Michael Graham, *Great Dechurching: Who's Leaving, Why Are They Going, and What Will It Take to Bring Them Back?* Zondervan, 2023.

[71] Melissa Deckman, Generation Z and Religion: What New Data Show, *Religion in Public: exploring the mix of sacred and secular*, February 10, 2020. Available: https://religioninpublic.blog/2020/02/10/generation-z-and-religion-what-new-data-show/#:~:text=When%20it%20comes%20to%20attendance%20at%20religious%20services%2C,1%20in%204%20report%20attending%20weekly%20or%20more.

[72] Sarah Skinner, Mind the Gap: Curated Reads for Gen Z—and their Z-Curious Colleagues, *McKinsey & Company*, 2022. Available: https://www.mckinsey.com/~/media/mckinsey/email/genz/2022/11/29/2022-11-29b.html.

[73] Sequoia Carrillo, U.S. reading and math scores drop to lowest level in decades, NPR, June 21, 2023. Available: https://www.npr.org/2023/06/21/1183445544/u-s-reading-and-math-scores-drop-to-lowest-level-in-decades.

[74] Xochitl Gonzalez, The Schools That Are No Longer Teaching Kids to Read Books, *The Atlantic*, June 19, 2024. Available: https://www.theatlantic.com/ideas/archive/2024/06/nyc-schools-stopped-teaching-books/678675/?utm_source=msn.

[75] Melissa Baron, What are the Actual Reading Trends for Gen Z? *Book Riot*, May 3, 2023. Available: https://bookriot.com/gen-z-reading-trends/#:~:text=Gen%20Z%20helped%20contribute%20to%20another%20great%20year,of%20sales%29%2C%20and%20hardcover

%20sales%20declined%20by%203%25.

[76] Steve Rabey, Enrollment Declines and Shifts Continue at Evangelical Seminaries, Ministry Watch, November 26, 2022. Available: https://ministrywatch.com/enrollment-declines-and-shifts-continue-at-evangelical-seminaries/.

[77] Tobin Grant, Why 1940's America wasn't as religious as you think—the rise and fall of American Religion. *Religious News Service*, December 11, 2014. Available: https://religionnews.com/2014/12/11/1940s-america-wasnt-religious-think-rise-fall-american-religion/.

[78] Jim Davis, Michael Graham, and Ryan Burge, *Great Dechurching: Who's Leaving, Why Are They Going, and What Will It Take to Bring Them Back?*, Zondervan, 2023.

[79] Jeffrey M. Jones, U.S. Church Membership Falls Below Majority for First Time, *Gallup*, March 29, 2021. Available: https://news.gallup.com/poll/341963/church-membership-falls-below-majority-first-time.aspx.

[80] Jeffrey M. Jones, U.S. Church Attendance Still Lower Than Pre-Pandemic, Gallup, June 26, 2023. Available: https://news.gallup.com/poll/507692/church-attendance-lower-pre-pandemic.aspx.

[81] Jeffrey M. Jones, Church Attendance Has Declined in Most U.S. Religious Groups: Three in 10 U.S. adults attend religious services regularly, led by Mormons at 67%. *Gallup.com, March 24, 2024. Available:* https://news.gallup.com/poll/642548/church-attendance-declined-religious-groups.aspx.

[82] Esteban Ospina and Max Roser, Marriages and Divorces: How is the institution of marriage changing? What percentage of marriages end in divorce? Explore global data on marriages and divorces. Our World in Data, April, 2024, Available: https://ourworldindata.org/marriages-and-divorces.

[83] Deidre McPhillips, US fertility rate dropped to lowest in a century as births dipped in 2023, CNN, April 25, 2024. Available: https://edition.cnn.com/2024/04/24/health/us-birth-rate-decline-2023-cdc/index.html.

[84] The Postwar Economy: 1945-1960, *American History: From Revolution to Reconstruction and beyond.* Available:

https://www.let.rug.nl/usa/outlines/history-1994/postwar-america/the-postwar-economy-1945-1960.php.

[85] Now known as Cru.

[86]Timeline of Historic Events, Billy Graham Evangelistic Association, Available: https://billygraham.org/news/media-resources/electronic-press-kit/bgea-history/timeline-of-historic-events/.

[87] John Dart, Billy Graham Recalls Help From Hearst, *Los Angeles Times*, June 7, 1997. Available: https://www.latimes.com/archives/la-xpm-1997-06-07-me-1034-story.html.

[88] Molly Worthen, Evangelical Boilerplate: Billy Graham's Innocuous blend of showmanship and salvation, *The Nation, February 4, 2015. Available: https://www.thenation.com/article/archive/evangelical-boilerplate/.*

[89] Billy Graham: A New Kind of Evangelist, *Time,* Monday, Oct. 25, 1954. Available: https://content.time.com/time/subscriber/article/0,33009,823597-1,00.html.

[90] Molly Worthen, Evangelical Boilerplate: Billy Graham's Innocuous blend of showmanship and salvation, *The Nation, February 4, 2015. Available: https://www.thenation.com/article/archive/evangelical-boilerplate/.*

[91] Oral Roberts Dies: Funeral Arrangements Pending for Legendary Evangelist, December 15, 2009. Available: https://web.archive.org/web/20091222070102/http://static.ktul.com/documents/oralroberts.pdf; Harrell, Jr., David Edwin (1985). *Oral Roberts: An American Life.* Bloomington, IN: Indiana University Press.

[92] D. E. Harrell, All Things are Possible: The Healing and Charismatic Revivals in Modern America. Indiana University Press, 1978.

[93] What is the Latter Rain Movement? Bibliatodo, June 20, 2024. Available: https://www.bibliatodo.com/En/christian-reflections/what-is-the-latter-rain-movement/. For a full treatment, see D. E. Harrell, All Things are Possible: The Healing and Charismatic Revivals in Modern America. Indiana University Press, 1978.Richard M. Riss, Latter Rain: *The Latter Rain Movement of 1948 and the **Mid-T**wentieth*

*Century Evangelical Awakening,* Honeycomb Visual Productions, 1987.

[94] Joshua R. Ziefle, "The Place of Pentecost: David Johannes du Plessis, the Assemblies of God, and the Development of Ecumenical Pentecostalism." PhD Dissertation submitted to Princeton Theological Seminary, 2010. Available: https://archives.northwestu.edu/bitstream/handle/nu/55303/Ziefle_Joshua_DPhil_2010.pdf?sequence=1.

[95] Du Plessis, David (1970). *The Spirit bade me go: the astounding move of God in the denominational churches* (2005 ed.). Bridge-Logos. For those who may not know understand the Pentecostal doctrine of Baptism in the Holy Spirit, the phrase first appears in the Bible (in all four gospels) in the message of John the Baptist: "I baptize you in water, but he will baptize you in the Holy Spirit" (Mark 1:8). The phrase appears again when Jesus, before his ascension, declares to the disciples that they should not leave Jerusalem but rather, wait to be "baptized in the Holy Spirit. (Acts 1:5). All interpreters would agree that this promise was fulfilled in Acts 2:4: "All of them were filled with the Holy Spirit and began to speak in other tongues as the Spirit enabled them." The Pentecostal Movement sprang from the belief that speaking in tongues continues to evidence the baptism in the Holy Spirit, just as it did for the disciples on the Day of Pentecost, and it quickly spread around the world, growing to hundreds of millions of adherents.

[96] Larry Christenson, Bennett, Dennis Joseph (1917-91) and Rita (1934). In Stanley M. Burgess (ed.), The new international Dictionary of Pentecostal and Charismatic Movements (Ed. Rev. and exp.), Zondervan, 2002, 369-371.

[97] Dianne Kirby, The Cold War and American Religion, *Oxford Research Encyclopedias*, May 24, 2027. Available: https://doi.org/10.1093/acrefore/9780199340378.013.398.

[98] President-Elect Says Soviet Demoted Zhukov Because of Their Friendship, *New York Times*, Dec 23, 1952. Available: https://timesmachine.nytimes.com/timesmachine/1952/12/23/84381128.html?pageNumber=1.

[99] William I. Hitchcock, How Dwight Eisenhower Found God in the White House: Dwight Eisenhower and Billy Graham shaped a half-century of religion in America. *History*, May 10, 2023. Available: https://www.history.com/

news/eisenhower-billy-graham-religion-in-god-we-trust.

[100] Robert Trexler and Jennifer Trafton. C.S. Lewis: Did You Know? *Christian History 88*, 2005. *Available: https://christianhistoryinstitute.org/magazine/article/ lewis-reality-did-you-know.*

[101] Religion: Faith for a Lenten Age, *Time*, March 8, 1948. Available: https://content.time.com/

time/covers/0,16641,19480308,00.html.

[102] Religion: To Be or Not to Be, *Time*, March 16, 1959. Available: https://time.com/archive/6870089/religion-to-be-orr-not-to-be/.

[103] Religion: Witness to an Ancient Truth, Time, April 20, 1962. Available: https:time.com/archive/6811204/religion-witness-to-and-ancient-truth/.

[104] "Is God Dead?", *Time*, April 8, 1966. Available:

https://time.com/archive/6629149/is-god-dead/.

**[105]** A Penitential Order: Rite One, *The (Online) Book of Common Prayer*, *The Church Hymnal Corporation*, 2007. Available: https://bcponline.org.

[106] Adrian Fortescue, "Confiteor:" In Charles Herbermann (ed.) *Catholic Encyclopedia*, Vol 4. Robert Appleton Company, 1908.

[107] For those who may be concerned that I am declaring belief here in the Calvinist concept the persistence of the saints, or "once saved, always saved," I would answer that I believe Christians can commit apostasy and lose their salvation, but such a loss cannot occur casually.

[108] Jack Deere, Surprised by the Power of the Spirit, Zondervan, 1993, 54

[109] For a full discussion, see Liam Jerrold Fraser, The Secret Sympathy: New Atheism, Protestant Fundamentalism, and Evolution, *Open Theology*, 2005, 1:445-454.

[110] Sarah Hinlicky Wilson, Lament for a Divided Church, *Christianity Today*, March 17,

2014. Available: https://www.christianitytoday.com/ct/2014/march/lament-for-divided-church.html.

[111] Clive Staples Lewis, *Mere Christianity*. Zondervan, 2001. Available: https://genius.com/C-s-lewis-mere-christianity-preface-annotated.

[112] Rudolph Otto, *The Idea of the Holy: At Inquiry into the non-rational factor in the idea of the divine and its relation to the rational*, trans. By John W. Harvey, Oxford University Press, 1950.

[113] Otto, 136.

[114] Kenneth Grahame, *The Wind in the Willows*. Oxford University Press, 2010. Available: https://www.gutenberg.org/files/289/289-h/289-h.htm#chap01.

[115] Lewis, C. S., & Whitfield, R. (1946). *The great divorce*. New York: Macmillan.

[116] Joseph Castleberry, *The Kingdom Net: Learning to Network Like Jesus*. My Healthy Church, 2012.

[117] Pope Francis explains 'who am I to judge' in his new book, Catholic News Agency, Jan 12, 2016. Available: https://www.catholicnewsagency.com/news/33231/pope-francis-explains-who-am-i-to-judge-in-

his-new-book .

[118] Homer, *The Odyssey*, c. 800 BC. Available: https://classics.mit.edu/Homer/odyssey.html.

[119] Kristen Bialik, Key facts about race and marriage, 50 years after Loving v. Virginia, *Pew Research Center*, June 12, 2017. Available: https://www.pewresearch.org/short-reads/2017/06/12/key-facts-about-race-and-marriage-50-years-after-loving-v-virginia/; *Kim Parker and Amanda Barrasso, In Vice President Kamala Harris, we can see how America has changed*, Pew Research Center, *February* 25, 2021. *Available: https://* www.pewresearch.org/short-reads/2021/02/25/in-vice-president-kamala-harris-we-can-see-how-america-has-changed/.

[120] Justin McCarthy, U.S. Approval of Interracial

Marriage at New High of 94%, September 10, 2021. Available: https://www.news.gallup.com/poll/354638/approval-interracial-marriage-new-high.aspx/.

[121] Richard Stearns, *The Hole in our Gospel: What does God Expect of Us? The answer that changed my life and might just change the world*. Thomas Nelson Inc, 2009.

[122] Tennessee governor signs bill calling for 30 days of prayer and fasting in July, *Lifesite News*, Jun 20, 2024. Available: https://www.lifesitenews.com/news/tennessee-governor-signs-bill-calling-for-30-days-of-prayer-and-fasting-in-july/.

[123] Tennessee General Assembly, House Joint Resolution 803, February 7, 2024. Available: https://www.capitol.tn.gov/Bills/113/Bill/HJR0803.pdf.

[124] Áron Buzási, Paul Ricœur and the Idea of Second Naivety: Origins, Analogues, Applications, *Etudes Ricoeuriennes*, Vol. 13 No. 2 (2022). Available: https://ricoeur.pitt.edu/ojs/ricoeur/issue/view/28.

[125] Darrin J. Rodgers, This Week in AG History, Dec. 11, 1960. Ag.org, December 12, 2019. Available: https://news.ag.org/en/article-repository/news/2019/12/this-week-in-ag-history----dec-11-1960.

[126] Earl Creps, *Reverse Mentoring: How Young Leaders Can Transform the Church and Why We Should Let Them*. (Jossey-Bass Leadership Network Series Book 26), Wiley, 2008.

[127] Procrustes was a figure in Greek mythology who tortured people by stretching them or cutting off their legs in order to make them fit onto an iron bed. The phrase "procrustean bed" refers to conceptual structure that may be imposed on a situation to make facts fit what the interpreter wants to make of them, despite whatever distortions of reality the argument may render.

Made in the USA
Middletown, DE
02 September 2024